MW01234910

Our Faith Journey Through Cancer

Velinda L Moore

*To Angela:
Peace, grace,
and mercy.*

Velinda L Moore

Copyright Notices:

NKJV

Scripture quotations marked (NKJV) are taken from the New King James Version®. Copyright © 1982 by Thomas Nelson. Used by permission. All rights reserved.

NCV

Scripture quotations marked (NCV) are taken from the New Century Version®. Copyright © 2005 by Thomas Nelson. Used by permission. All rights reserved.

NIV

Scripture quotations marked (NIV) are taken from the Holy Bible, New International Version®, NIV®. Copyright © 1973, 1978, 1984, 2011 by Biblica, Inc.™ Used by permission of Zondervan. All rights reserved worldwide. www.zondervan.com The "NIV" and "New International Version" are trademarks registered in the United States Patent and Trademark Office by Biblica, Inc.™

Copyright © 2016 Velinda Moore
All rights reserved.
ISBN: 1514788357
ISBN-13: 978-1514788356

DEDICATION

To my husband, my soul-mate, my best friend - Albert Taylor Moore. The ride was shorter than I would have hoped, but it was also more awesome than I could have ever imagined.

To my nieces, Velinda and Shawna. Your faith, strength, encouragement and support helped me to keep moving in the transition to my own journey. I could not love you more if you had come from my own womb. I am very proud of the women you have become.

ACKNOWLEDGMENTS

My Family
(especially Dad, Mom, Julie, Brad and Roger)
Pastor Dave
Zach
Pastor Leo
Martha
The doctors and staff of RCC, Wakefield
Marine Corp League Detachment 1257, NC
American Legion Post 52, NC
Transitions LifeCare, Raleigh, NC.

INTRODUCTION

You may ask, as I have asked myself, why am I writing this? This was not an easy journey; it was however a very blessed journey. My husband and I both experienced a lot of growth and a lot of change. I am not at all the same person that I was prior to this journey. God often uses people who have travelled the journey to walk beside and encourage others who start down a similar path. I pray that God will use me and all that He has taught me over the past almost 2 years, that I may be a blessing to others.

Please know that I am not a Bible Scholar or Expert. I have no Seminary or other formal training. I do not set out to analyze scripture here. What I present in these pages is a look back at the journey and the importance of God's word during that journey. I do walk through specific scripture passages that were key to us at different moments along the journey.

This book is also part of my healing. It is often extremely difficult to see growth in the midst of the storm. By stepping back and working through it, going back through my journals and back through the scripture that each of us marked in our bibles, I see the path behind me more clearly. I see the awesome God that I serve, how He directed our steps, and the wonderful people who God put in our path for our comfort, support and growth.

What are the three most important things that I have learned through this journey? All three come from a passage very familiar to most people -

Psalm 23:4 (NKJV)

4 Yea, though I walk through the valley of the shadow of death,
I will fear no evil;
For You are with me;
Your rod and Your staff, they comfort me.

One of the key words in this passage is the word "through". God intends for us to walk through the valley. He does not want us to stop and setup a homestead there. We need to keep walking, to keep moving forward. How can God direct your steps if you aren't taking any?

The second key word in this passage is the word "shadow". It is impossible to have a shadow without a light source. Standing in the shade, you may not feel the sun. The fact that there is shade, that some object is casting a shadow, is direct proof that the sun is still there whether you feel it or not. The same is true of God when we journey through the various valleys of shadows. You may not always feel His presence, yet the dark shadow is direct evidence that He is still present.

Thirdly, neither valleys nor shadows go on forever. There is a border for every shadow; when you step out of the shadow the light is immediately present. Likewise, all valleys have borders. The very definition of a valley is "a depression or low area of land between uplands, hills or mountains, typically following the path of a river or stream." During these journeys, Jesus, the water of life flows through our valley.

John 4:13-14 (NIV)

13 Jesus answered, "Everyone who drinks this water will be thirsty again, 14 but whoever drinks the water I give them will never thirst. Indeed, the water I give them will become in them a spring of water welling up to eternal life."

And finally, the only way out of the valley is to scale to the top of the mountain. That is an awesome image.

OUR FAITH JOURNEY TOGETHER: THE DIAGNOSIS

I remember the night we first received the diagnosis very clearly. Taylor had been experiencing some odd symptoms and we were concerned, but not afraid. He was generally healthy; his exam and all of his blood work results had been good at his physical less than a year earlier. Taylor had gone to the urgent care clinic that morning with a headache that was affecting his vision. His pain and the visual disturbance were bad enough that he asked a neighbor to drive him there. The doctor at the urgent care called ahead with her report and sent Taylor to the Hospital Emergency room. He called me at work and I met him at the ER.

When I arrived at the hospital they were ready to start doing a whole bunch of tests to figure out exactly what was wrong. We were informed that they didn't want to talk about it with us until they found the root cause, and also that this situation was way more than a headache and the prognosis was not good.

Later that evening, the ER doctor came to talk to us. His words made no sense. Taylor had a headache. How could we leap from Migraine or maybe a mini-stroke to Metastatic Cancer? This couldn't be happening. I suggested to the doctor several other things that could cause the same symptoms. We needed more tests, more biopsies, other things in this age of advanced medicine. Dr. Adams said, as kindly as he could, "One of my jobs is to give you an appropriate level of hope. I would be doing you a disservice to let you believe something that is not true. There are some treatments, some interventions, so there is hope for improvement. There is, however, no hope that this isn't an advanced and very complex cancer." His manner was very kind and very direct at the same time; for that I was, and still am, extremely thankful.

The next discussion between Taylor and I was - What did we know for sure? The preliminary scans showed it was a stage IV cancer. It had already metastasized to at least three secondary locations. We did not know yet which of the four sites was the primary cancer site. We did know there was currently no curative treatment for stage IV cancer with multiple metastases regardless of the primary type.

Next topic - Who do we tell, how and when? Taylor had concerns about being treated differently, being pitied. Yet there were some who needed to know soon; we would need a support structure and a prayer team to stand with us. Who could we trust to keep this private for now? Who did we trust with our spiritual welfare at this difficult moment? Who did we need to be certain would hear this news directly from us?

Our nieces, who we have been very close with us all of their lives, needed to know. Taylor could not bear the thought that they would hear this news second hand; it absolutely had to come from us. They were both in college, they were adults now. How information like this is framed and communicated is very important. Taylor was going to be in the hospital for a while as they battled the brain swelling and did even more tests. It was decided that I should get the girls together and tell them both at the same time. It had to be in person and there needed to be a time for questions.

I prayed long and hard that night for guidance. I was led to tell them the diagnosis and then to lead off the discussion with reading Psalm 139:13-16 and saying "...so in some ways everything had changed, and in some ways absolutely nothing had. God was still going to call Uncle Taylor home on the same day He ordained before Taylor was born. We were now just much more aware that there was a last day and that it was probably sooner than we had originally thought".

Psalm 139:13-16 (NIV)

13 For you created my inmost being;
you knit me together in my mother's womb.
14 I praise you because I am fearfully and wonderfully made;
your works are wonderful; I know that full well.
15 My frame was not hidden from you
when I was made in the secret place,
when I was woven together in the depths of the earth.
16 Your eyes saw my unformed body;
all the days ordained for me were written in your book
before one of them came to be.

As a family we came back to this truth repeatedly over many months. I printed it on index cards and placed them around the house and my office. God was still in control. Only God knew the number of days that Taylor would have. The doctors and other specialists had highly educated opinions based on their training and experience. We needed to consider that information, but not fully accept it as truth. God could choose to perform a miracle. Maybe Taylor would be one of the outliers that survived for 5 or even 10 years. That was completely up to God. Another verse that reiterates this truth is found in Job.

Job 14:5 (NIV)

5 A person's days are determined; you have decreed the number of his months and have set limits he cannot exceed.

All we could do was trust God, stay positive and pray for God to lead us, and the doctors. I prayed also that God would purposely put two sets of people in our lives at this time - Believers of strong faith to stand and pray with us and encourage us, and non-believers or those struggling in faith to witness what God was going to accomplish through this diagnosis and whatever time we had left.

STAYING POSITIVE IN FAITH

No matter how strong your faith is, news like this rocks you to your core. We had to stay strong; we had to stay positive. Negativity is so very draining. We had been so blessed all of our lives together. We couldn't turn our backs on all of that at this time. God was still in control. A passage from Job reminds us of this truth.

Job 2:10 (NIV)

10 Job answered, "You are talking like a foolish woman. Should we take only good things from God and not trouble?" In spite of all this Job did not sin in what he said.

We had been the encouragers to so many people before this. Plus, God answered my prayer to place skeptics and questioners in our path and to give us the wisdom and words to be a strong witness of all God had done and all that He was doing now. I became very aware of so many people watching us. "Where is your God now?" We had to be grounded, positive, and stay strong in our faith, now more than ever. We needed to lift the questioners, not allow ourselves to be dragged down into doubt and skepticism.

I started reading the Bible aloud for us as Taylor's eye sight was still being affected. I prayed that God would give us a word of encouragement, a passage or two to cling to as we moved forward. These, and the one above, became central to us as we accepted the diagnosis and moved forward.

2 Timothy 1:7-12 (NIV)

7 For the Spirit God gave us does not make us timid, but gives us power, love and self-discipline. 8 So do not be ashamed of the testimony about our Lord or of me his prisoner. Rather, join with me in suffering for the gospel, by the power of God. 9 He has saved us and called us to a holy life—not because of anything we have done but because of his own purpose and grace. This grace was given us in Christ Jesus before the beginning of time, 10 but it has now been revealed through the appearing of our Savior, Christ Jesus, who has destroyed death and has brought life and immortality to light through the gospel. 11 And of this gospel I was appointed a herald and an apostle and a teacher. 12 That is why I am suffering as I am. Yet this is no cause for shame, because I know whom I have believed, and am convinced that he is able to guard what I have entrusted to Him until that day.

God never promised us an easy journey. He did promise to strengthen us for the journey He chooses for us.

HELP ALWAYS COMES, BUT NOT ALWAYS FROM WHERE YOU EXPECT

If anyone were to ask you at this moment, right now, "If you had a dire need, which of your friends do you absolutely know would be there to help?", most people would have a list that immediately comes to mind. Maybe the list contains a few people with whom you have a long history. Perhaps, the list in your mind contains people who you helped through a rough patch at some point in the past. We started out being open with that small circle of friends. We were quickly disappointed when a number of those people that we were absolutely sure would rally around us did not. We felt betrayed and hurt. We cried out to God. Why?

One day during this early period I remembered something I had told so many people when they were struggling in some area – "There is nothing that you are struggling with that Jesus did not experience as a man." OK, sure, Jesus was betrayed by one of the twelve but we felt let down by a higher percentage of friends than 8%. Jesus still had 92% of His inner circle standing with Him in His time of greatest need. Or did He?

Mark 14:32-41 (NKJV)

32 Then they came to a place which was named Gethsemane; and He said to His disciples, "Sit here while I pray." 33 And He took Peter, James, and John with Him, and He began to be troubled and deeply distressed. 34 Then He said to them, "My soul is exceedingly sorrowful, even to death. Stay here and watch."

35 He went a little farther, and fell on the ground, and prayed that if it were possible, the hour might pass from Him. 36 And He said, "Abba, Father, all things are possible for You. Take this cup away from Me; nevertheless, not what I will, but what You will."

37 Then He came and found them sleeping, and said to Peter, "Simon, are you sleeping? Could you not watch one hour? 38 Watch and pray, lest you enter into temptation. The spirit indeed is willing, but the flesh is weak."

39 Again He went away and prayed, and spoke the same words. 40 And when He returned, He found them asleep again, for their eyes were heavy; and they did not know what to answer Him.

41 Then He came the third time and said to them, "Are you still sleeping and resting? It is enough! The hour has come; behold, the Son of Man is being betrayed into the hands of sinners. 42 Rise, let us be going. See, My betrayer is at hand."

When Jesus was "exceedingly sorrowful, even to death", He asked three of His most trusted to just be with Him. His life hung in the balance, He knew the pain and suffering that would soon come to Him. And His trusted inner circle slept. How could we expect more from our inner circle? We had to lean on God as our provider. God uses people to provide for our needs; He gets to choose those people, not us.

We hit a point where it was obvious that Taylor's health was not good. His weight loss, pale color and eventual hair loss told everyone that there was something seriously wrong. It was at this point that we started really sharing with all of our friends and acquaintances what was really going on. It was shocking at first the number of people that rallied around us. These were not necessarily the people that we were positive would be our 100% dependable inner circle. That didn't matter. God provided in His way, in His time.

We were reminded to ask God for help, to depend on Him. People are just imperfect humans and do disappoint;

I, myself, am an imperfect human. Our center of trust has to be in our Heavenly Father, not in His fallible children.

WHY ME? WHY IS THIS HAPPENING TO US?

I distinctly remember the night Taylor first expressed to me a deep struggle many people have experienced. It was several months after the diagnosis when he turned to me and said "Darling, why me? Why us? Why is this happening to us? I keep trying to figure out what I have done wrong. Is God punishing me for something?" I think he was taken aback when I responded "Why not us? All over the earth right now people are getting diagnosed with cancers and other horrible diseases. People are going through a vast array of trials and sufferings. We live in a fallen world. God never promised us an easy life; He did promise to walk with us and that something good can come from all of the bad.".

We spent the next few days working through the passages below. We routinely went back to these throughout the journey.

1 Peter 5:6-11 (NIV)

6 Humble yourselves, therefore, under God's mighty hand, that he may lift you up in due time. 7 Cast all your anxiety on Him because he cares for you. 8 Be alert and of sober mind. Your enemy the devil prowls around like a roaring lion looking for someone to devour. 9 Resist him, standing firm in the faith, because you know that the family of believers throughout the world is undergoing the same kind of sufferings. 10 And the God of all grace, who called you to his eternal glory in Christ, after you have suffered a little while, will himself restore you and make you strong, firm and steadfast. 11 To Him be the power forever and ever. Amen.

Verse 7 can be the most challenging of this passage. I would be lying outright if I said there was not an increase in anxiety. At one point we were both on anti-anxiety medications. Continuously repeating to myself "God's got this!" was very important to maintaining my sanity. Read the passage carefully again. God did not say "you will not have anxiety" or "anxiety is some sort of sinful doubt". God knows us. He made us and he knew we would have anxiety in situations like this. His call is to not dwell or drown in the anxiety, but rather to "cast all your anxiety on Him"[1]

Psalm 13 (NIV)

1 How long, Lord? Will you forget me forever?
How long will you hide your face from me?
2 How long must I wrestle with my thoughts
and day after day have sorrow in my heart?
How long will my enemy triumph over me?
3 Look on me and answer, Lord my God.
Give light to my eyes, or I will sleep in death,
4 and my enemy will say, "I have overcome him,"
and my foes will rejoice when I fall.
5 But I trust in your unfailing love;
my heart rejoices in your salvation.
6 I will sing the Lord's praise,
for he has been good to me.

I think a normal response to any debilitating disease is to, at least at first, cry out to God for healing. Perfect healing, and that alone, can be the only valid answer to crying out to God. Then we feel like God is hiding; Why am I not healed? The truth is that none of us were ever

---

[1] *While I did not see it at this point in the journey, Verse 10 would become very important and very true for me after Taylor's death.*

intended to live forever in this world. Sometimes God is answering and we have to be accepting to hearing that the answer is not what our first choice would be.

Psalm 61 (NIV)

1 Hear my cry, O God; listen to my prayer.

2 From the ends of the earth I call to you,

I call as my heart grows faint;

lead me to the rock that is higher than I.

3 For you have been my refuge, a strong tower against the foe.

4 I long to dwell in your tent forever

and take refuge in the shelter of your wings.

Romans 8:28 (NCV) [2]

28 We know that in everything God works for the good of those who love Him. They are the people he called, because that was his plan.

---

[2] *You will find scripture quoted from 3 different versions in this book. Taylor's eye sight was really suffering because of the progression of the brain lesions, so he was soon unable to read from his NIV version. My parents found him a very nice, very large print Bible. As it was a New King James Version, most reading and notes moved to NKJV. I began reading to him aloud on days that even the large print proved too challenging. Sometimes that was from my NIV, other times from the NCV Study Bible we received as a gift from Pastor Dave.*

We saw so much good come from this journey. Even as I typed that previous sentence now, I admit it feels VERY weird to express that good came from my husband's physical suffering and death. Yet, it is very true. We saw people come to faith, we witnessed people discovery mercy and forgiveness. God was working mightily in this situation. God's plan is perfect and He desires good things for us.

FROM FACT TO FAITH

I struggled with a title for this section. I also considered "The Transfer from Head to Heart" and "The Transition from Fact to Truth". The key here is that there is a great chasm between intellectual knowledge and spiritual faith. Even Satan has intellectual knowledge of who Jesus is and what he did; the danger is when you stop short of trusting that information with your whole self, your whole heart and your eternity.

Taylor had a struggle in his faith about mid-way through treatment. We had to deal with and accept that there was no curative treatment available. Without God Himself touching Taylor and healing him directly, this cancer would end his life. The best we could hope for in medical intervention was to buy more time, to slow down the progression.

As I sensed his inner struggles, we talked at length about faith. We began reading the Bible together often. I asked him directly one day, "Honey, you know where you are going at the end of this journey, right? In your heart-of-hearts, you know the answer, right? I need to know that you know." Taylor had been a professing believer for many, many years. He had been baptized. He had attended church and Bible study. He had encouraged others in their faith. It was so hard to see him struggle.

His response startled me at first. "Darling, I know in my head. I know who God is. I know who Jesus is and what He has done for us, for me. I know all of the facts, all of the stories. I know I can call on God and have said I trust Him to respond. At this moment, I have to go from knowing... thinking... that I can call on God, that I can trust Him, to actually calling on Him and putting my whole self - my life and my death in His hands. My head believes, but my heart is troubled. My heart is doubting what I know to be true. I am scared. Have I done enough? Have I believed strong enough? Why does my heart doubt?"

I remembered reading an explanation of this type of struggle once. I believe I read it in one of the C.S. Lewis non-fiction books. Paraphrasing from memory – It is one thing to trust a piece of rope to secure a few boxes. It is something entirely different to trust that same piece of rope to dangle you over the abyss. You only really know how much you believe when that trust is a matter of life and death.

I counseled him that there were only two things that he needed to do - Believe and Receive. Believe in the truth of the Gospel and Accept the gift of Grace. He said he had the belief part down, we needed to work together on his full acceptance of the gift of a Salvation that he did not deserve, of the gift of Grace. Grace, after all, is God's Redemption at Christ's Expense.[3] As we talked through this, I strongly remember the image of Taylor dropping to his knees on the kitchen floor, crying. Soon he was sprawled out on his belly on the kitchen floor. I grabbed some materials his pastor-friend Leo had given him months earlier and sat on the floor beside him and read through them aloud. A while later he called Leo and another friend - Zach - and asked them to come to the house and talk with him. Taylor had read the Bible in church, small groups, Bible studies and the like throughout his walk with God. He became very hungry at a whole

3 I'm sure that many of you have seen Grace as "God's Riches at Christ's Expense". I have never been a fan of that wording. Christ died and was resurrected for our Salvation, for our Redemption, not for any riches. If you are on a Faith Journey for riches, you may need to step back and reconsider your motivation.

new level to hear the Word from that moment until his last breath. He had a new peace in his heart about what was to come.

GOD SENDS COMFORTERS

I need to reiterate here that I am not a theologian. I am merely a Christian woman trying to find my way in this world. I do not understand everything, nor am I meant to understand everything now.

1 Corinthians 13:12 (NCV)

12 It is the same with us. Now we see a dim reflection, as if we were looking into a mirror, but then we shall see clearly. Now I know only a part, but then I will know fully, as God has known me.

The purpose of this book is to write about what happened as we went through the journey. Whether these comforters were angels, the spirits of the actual people, or something else could be debated by many learned theologians. I have not had an angel engage me in

26

conversation; I do however believe it is possible. There are many places in the Bible when an angel appears and/or speaks to individuals. Why God would send angels/comforters to Taylor is not for me to know or understand. First in this chapter I will share the scriptures that helped me as I watched Taylor and as he shared things that had been shared with him. The second part of the chapter will address the instances that I documented in my journal as they happened.

****

The first scripture that I knew involves Moses and Elijah appearing before Jesus and some of the apostles. I suppose if God could enable them to appear on earth, He could enable anyone that would be a comfort to us to appear.

Mark 9:2-8 (NCV)

2 Six days later, Jesus took Peter, James, and John up on a high mountain by themselves. While they watched, Jesus' appearance was changed. 3 His clothes became shining white, whiter than any person could make them. 4 Then Elijah and Moses appeared to them, talking with Jesus.

5 Peter said to Jesus, "Teacher, it is good that we are here. Let us make three tents—one for you, one for Moses, and one for Elijah." 6 Peter did not know what to say, because he and the others were so frightened. 7 Then a cloud came and covered them, and a voice came from the cloud, saying, "This is my Son, whom I love. Listen to Him!"

8 Suddenly Peter, James, and John looked around, but they saw only Jesus there alone with them.

Reading and studying further, I found many other examples of where the Bible addresses angels appearing and communicating with His people. I list a few of them here.

Joshua 5:13-15 (NCV)

13 Joshua was near Jericho when he looked up and saw a man standing in front of him with a sword in his hand. Joshua went to him and asked, "Are you a friend or an enemy?"

14 The man answered, "I am neither. I have come as the commander of the Lord's army."

Then Joshua bowed facedown on the ground and asked, "Does my master have a command for me, his servant?"

15 The commander of the Lord's army answered, "Take off your sandals, because the place where you are standing is holy." So Joshua did.

There are many times in the Bible when an angel appears to a woman to predict a birth. I think everyone knows the references in the new testament to the angel appearing separately to both Mary and Joseph and also to Zechariah (John the Baptist's father). I also like the story of the angel appearing to Sampson's parents.

Judges 13:2-21 (NCV)

2 There was a man named Manoah from the tribe of Dan, who lived in the city of Zorah. He had a wife, but she could not have children. 3 The angel of the Lord appeared to Manoah's wife and said, "You have not been able to have children, but you will become pregnant and give birth to a son. 4 Be careful not to drink wine or beer or eat anything that is unclean, 5 because you will become pregnant and have a son. You must never cut his hair, because he will be a Nazirite, given to God from birth. He will begin to save Israel from the power of the Philistines."

6 Then Manoah's wife went to him and told him what had happened. She said, "A man from God came to me. He looked like an angel from God; his appearance was frightening. I didn't ask him where he was from, and he didn't tell me his name. 7 But he said to me, 'You will become pregnant and will have a son. Don't drink wine or beer or eat anything that is unclean, because the boy will be a Nazirite to God from his birth until the day of his death.'"

8 Then Manoah prayed to the Lord: "Lord, I beg you to let the man of God come to us again. Let him teach us what we should do for the boy who will be born to us."

9 God heard Manoah's prayer, and the angel of God came to Manoah's wife again while she was sitting in the field. But her husband Manoah was not with her. 10 So she ran to tell him, "He is here! The man who appeared to me the other day is here!"

11 Manoah got up and followed his wife. When he came to the man, he said, "Are you the man who spoke to my wife?" The man said, "I am."

12 So Manoah asked, "When what you say happens, what kind of life should the boy live? What should he do?"

13 The angel of the Lord said, "Your wife must be careful to do everything I told her to do. 14 She must not eat anything that grows on a grapevine, or drink any wine or beer, or eat anything that is unclean. She must do everything I have commanded her."

15 Manoah said to the angel of the Lord, "We would like you to stay awhile so we can cook a young goat for you."

16 The angel of the Lord answered, "Even if I stay awhile, I would not eat your food. But if you want to prepare something, offer a burnt offering to the Lord." (Manoah did not understand that the man was really the angel of the Lord.)

17 Then Manoah asked the angel of the Lord, "What is your name? Then we will honor you when what you have said really happens."

18 The angel of the Lord said, "Why do you ask my name? It is too amazing for you to understand." 19 So Manoah sacrificed a young goat on a rock and offered some grain as a gift to the Lord. Then an amazing thing happened as Manoah and his wife watched. 20 The flames went up to the sky from the altar. As the fire burned, the angel of the Lord went up to heaven in the flame. When Manoah and his wife saw that, they bowed facedown on the ground. 21 The angel of the Lord did not appear to them again. Then Manoah understood that the man was really the angel of the Lord.

Lest you think angels are only an old testament occurrence, or at least only occurred before Jesus' birth. There are several more references in the new testament. You can do your own exhaustive study if you'd like. Here is one more from Acts; this is the last one I will share at this point.

Acts 10:1-7 (NIV)

1 At Caesarea there was a man named Cornelius, a centurion in what was known as the Italian Regiment. 2 He and all his family were devout and God-fearing; he gave generously to those in need and prayed to God regularly. 3 One day at about three in the afternoon he had a vision. He distinctly saw an angel of God, who came to him and said, "Cornelius!"

31

4 Cornelius stared at him in fear. "What is it, Lord?" he asked. The angel answered, "Your prayers and gifts to the poor have come up as a memorial offering before God. 5 Now send men to Joppa to bring back a man named Simon who is called Peter. 6 He is staying with Simon the tanner, whose house is by the sea."

7 When the angel who spoke to him had gone, Cornelius called two of his servants and a devout soldier who was one of his attendants. 8 He told them everything that had happened and sent them to Joppa.

****

My point in this chapter is that God sent this comfort to us according to His purpose. I only know what I witnessed, which included Taylor relaying to me what he had heard. When this happened it usually included Taylor using words and phrases I had never heard him use before.

The first time it happened, I was getting out of the shower when I heard Taylor in the living room talking to someone. When I came into the room to see who had stopped by to visit, only Taylor was present. I asked him, "Honey, who were you talking to?" He replied "My Uncle Albert…. (long pause) … which makes absolutely no sense since he died before I was born."

A few weeks later, Taylor had a pulmonary embolism and we almost lost him. We spent several days in the hospital. He was really scared for a while during that time. He fought off sleep as if he was afraid that if he fell asleep he would not wake up again. One morning I left the hospital room for a bit to go down the hall and get myself a cup of coffee (and a break). When I returned, Taylor seemed more at peace than I had seen him in many weeks. I asked him how he was feeling. He responded "I saw the guy with the dark curly hair again. He told me "Don't be worried just yet. There is an epic battle going on. Lots of people love you and are all offering up prayers and petitions for you to stay here a while longer. I'm here to tell you that it has not yet been decided." My husband had never used the phrase "prayers and petitions" before. If he was hallucinating or dreaming I would expect him to use his own phrases and idioms. I do know that the comforter who became known only as "the guy with the dark curly hair" spoke to Taylor a lot over Taylor's last months on earth. Uncle Albert was also a big comfort to Taylor along with a few others.

The only comforting appearance that I actually got to see firsthand came the Friday night that Taylor told me he was done with pursuing any further treatment. We were in bed and I was praying that God would put a hedge around us during this difficult time. I asked God to protect us from discouraging thoughts and doubting of faith. When I opened my eyes, in the darkness of our bedroom, I saw eleven angles standing around the bed facing away from us. There were four standing shoulder to shoulder down my side of the bed, three at the bottom of the bed and four on Taylor's side of the bed. I have never had a more peaceful night's sleep than I did that night.

Another word of comfort was relayed to me second hand. My Mom told me that while she was talking with Taylor, he had told her that the end was coming soon. He said he knew that he was dying and he even knew who was coming for him when the time came. Mom responded "The angel of death?". Taylor told her "No Janet. Our God is not about death. He conquered death. Our God is about life and light. I was told that an angel of light will be here when it is my time to leave this world."

There were several others, some of which I feel are too personal to share here. At least one of these encounters that Taylor spoke of took me by a bit of surprise. I had a preconceived idea of what angels would sound like and how they would phrase things. Pastor Dave reminded me that a messenger from God would appear in a form that was comforting to the one the message was intended for and the words would be a phrasing comforting and familiar to that person. These messages of comfort were for Taylor, not me. I was blessed just to be informed of some of the messages.

TREATMENT IS NO LONGER WORKING... NOW WHAT?

I really respect Taylor's doctors for not only understanding, but also focusing our discussions on "Quality vs Quantity". In my experience, so many doctors believe that the ultimate goal is to keep the patient breathing for as long as possible. It is as if death is a defeat to the doctor. Death is a natural part of life. Taylor's Oncologist and his Primary Care doctor both truly understand that life involves more than just drawing in a breath. Living and Life are not direct synonyms. There is a line from an Eric Bogle song that really sums this up well – "Never knew there was worse things than dying"[4]. Our doctors focused on Quality of Living. The plan that we

[4] *"And The Band Played Waltzing Matilda" by Eric Bogle. Album: Scraps of Paper. Copyright 1983 Flying Fish Records, Inc.*

decided on with the doctors, was to do MRIs and CT Scans to get measurements from all of the metastatic sites as well as the primary site, complete four rounds of Chemotherapy, then take all the same measurements again. If the primary site and the majority of the metastatic sites were the same size or smaller, the Chemotherapy was working. If the primary site and the majority of the metastatic sites were growing and/or there were any new sites, then treatment was not working and we were done.

It was a Wednesday when we had the appointment to review the results. There were two new sites and most of the other sites had continued to progress. Per the plan, we were done with treatment. The doctor did discuss some continued treatment options, as he felt he needed to lay out all of the choices available to Taylor. That discussion, like those before it, quickly became centered on Quality vs Quantity of life. He counselled Taylor that this was not the day to make a final decision. He told Taylor to take a few days and pray and meditate on his decision; we would move forward as Taylor desired.

The hardest thing for me at this time was not voicing an opinion as to how Taylor should proceed. This decision was Taylor's to make and all I could do was assure him that I would back him in whatever decision he prayerfully made. I also told him that no matter which decision he made, it was absolutely the right decision. We would not look back and second guess or entertain "What if's?". This was Taylor's body, Taylor's life, Taylor's decision. I pray that if I am ever in a similar situation those around me will understand that for me.

When we returned home Wednesday morning, Taylor went into his garage. Except to come in to sleep and occasionally to get something to drink, he remained in the garage until Friday afternoon. After this time of prayer and meditation, he came back into the house and said to me "Darling, Paul asked God 3 times to take his ailment away. I have asked at least 3,000 time. It is not God's will for me. I am going to die. We have a limited amount of time left together here and a lot to get accomplished before I leave." He was re-energized on how we should proceed with the remainder of the time that God had allotted to him. He started a list of things that needed to be done while he was still able; my Marine prepared to complete his mission.

The scriptures that became most important to us as we planned for whatever time we had left together here were:

2 Corinthians 12:7-10 (NKJV)

7 And lest I should be exalted above measure by the abundance of the revelations, a thorn in the flesh was given to me, a messenger of Satan to buffet me, lest I be exalted above measure. 8 Concerning this thing I pleaded with the Lord three times that it might depart from me. 9 And He said to me, "My grace is sufficient for you, for My strength is made perfect in weakness." Therefore, most gladly I will rather boast in my infirmities, that the power of Christ may rest upon me. 10 Therefore I take pleasure in infirmities, in reproaches, in needs, in persecutions, in distresses, for Christ's sake. For when I am weak, then I am strong.

Psalm 118:24 (NKJV)

24 This is the day the Lord has made;
We will rejoice and be glad in it.

Ecclesiastes 8:15 (NIV)

15 So I commend the enjoyment of life, because there is nothing better for a person under the sun than to eat and drink and be glad. Then joy will accompany them in their toil all the days of the life God has given them under the sun.

Taylor had determined to enjoy every moment that he had left. He requested a Going Away Party to celebrate the life he had enjoyed thus far and the final preparations for Graduation from this world. I called some friends to help me plan the party he requested. We needed to get this done soon while he was still feeling well enough to enjoy it. The party came together in 3 weeks. Family and friends travelled in from hours away. We had close to 200 people attend the party.

The quote I remember most from this time - When someone would comment on how strong Taylor was in handling all of this, he would reply, "I am not strong, I am secure. There a big difference."

2 Corinthians 5:6-9 (NCV)

6 So we are always confident, knowing that while we are at home in the body we are absent from the Lord. 7 For we walk by faith, not by sight. 8 We are confident, yes, well pleased rather to be absent from the body and to be present with the Lord. 9 Therefore we make it our aim, whether present or absent, to be well pleasing to Him.

For me, I think that what I wrote at that time in my journal and in the photo album from his party sums it up very well:

I am so very proud of my husband and how he has handled this journey. I shouldn't be at all surprised because he has always been one to hit any situation head-on, full steam. That is my Marine. I am thankful for everyone who made this day so very special for us!

John 14:1-4 (NKJV)

1 Let not your heart be troubled; you believe in God, believe also in Me. 2 In My Father's house are many mansions; if it were not so, I would have told you. I go to prepare a place for you. 3 And if I go and prepare a place for you, I will come again and receive you to Myself; that where I am, there you may be also. 4 And where I go you know, and the way you know."

TAYLOR'S GOING AWAY PARTY

I already mentioned the Going Away Party that Taylor requested and we were able to pull off with the help of many friends. I want to share some of the love and humor that came out of that three-hour party. It was truly a celebration, just as Taylor had hoped it would be.

Taylor supervised what was to be on the invitation flyers. He had some cartoons to be used. One was of a Marine standing in uniform. There was a USMC Bulldog. Another drawing had a cross with a Bible and praying hands. He also included a racecar and a sticker image that said "If I'm riding I'm happy." The wording was dictated:

> You are hereby invited to a Celebration of the
> Life and Times of Taylor Moore.

> As time draws near, please stop by and bring your favorite memories and reminiscences to share during this time of celebration.
>
> The time to celebrate a life is before the end comes while the individual is still available to participate in the joy and activities.

We were able to use the gym at the church we had been attending. They put down some special mats so that we could have Taylor's motorcycle there with him. That was very special to him. Taylor sat in his transport chair beside the motorcycle for the majority of the party and let folks come to him. My cousin, Roger, was even able to get some great photo shots using the mirrors on the bike.

One thing that Taylor requested for the party was an "In Loving Memory" book for people to write in at the party. My Mom and Dad were able to find one with lots of pages and a different scripture verse on each page. Taylor put this book on a table, which was setup beside him, with a note that said:

> Please share a note or a memory or a funny story about how we met or something fun we have done together. This is for me for now. I hope it will also be a comfort to Velinda later on when I am not here to make her laugh or smile.

A friend was able to get a large sheet cake in the theme of Ice Age, which was Taylor's favorite animated movie series ever. One of our friends, who was helping with the food, quickly cut the section out of the cake with the acorn on in and put it aside for Taylor. Scrat and his escapades trying to capture the acorn were Taylor's favorite parts of the movies. When Taylor finally got to eat it later we were all amused by his attempts at Scrat noises. Unlike Scrat, Taylor was able to eat his acorn.

A large group of my friends from work attended the party and brought a very special gift. This was another way that God provided through the people around us. To understand the importance of this gift, I need to back up to the week after Taylor decided to stop treatment for a moment.

Taylor had listed several things he really wanted to do before he got too weak to do them. These were things like: See the ocean one more time, take a long weekend trip with each of our nieces, visit the NASCAR Hall of Fame in Charlotte, NC. We had already lost Taylor's income and I had dropped back to part-time by the time of the party. There was, however, no way I was going to tell my terminally ill husband that we couldn't afford these trips. We had a home equity line of credit with a zero balance and a few credit cards with no balance. I would return to work after he finished his journey and could pay it off eventually. It would just have to take whatever it had to take.

So the gift from my friends? A large envelope decorated with phrases like "Taylor's Fun Fund" that contained cash from donations from all of my office friends. I did not have to go into debt to fulfill Taylor's travel desires. A few of these coworker friends even helped me in the planning and setup of the trips.

The party was a huge blessing for Taylor. Several people shared with him how his faith and testimony had made a positive impact on their own journey. Too often people do not get to hear the positive impacts of their life on other people. It was a blessing to me also; I still get to sit and read the funny stories a few at a time. That book, as simple as it is, is something I will always treasure.

I know I said it before, but I'm going to say it again – A huge Thank You to everyone who helped to organize and pull off the party and to all of those who took the time to attend.

THE DECISION FOR ME TO GO ON AN INDEFINITE UNPAID LEAVE

God was working all around us. We had so many opportunities to share our witness and God allowed us to observe the impact of His Plan. God would provide for our immediate needs. He had provided so many times already. We had to trust Him this time as well. God instructs us to "not worry". I had quoted this passage to others several times over the years. Now I needed to embrace it fully for myself.

Matthew 6:31-34 (NKJV)

31 "Therefore do not worry, saying, 'What shall we eat?' or 'What shall we drink?' or 'What shall we wear?' 32 For after all these things the Gentiles seek. For your heavenly Father knows that you need all these things. 33 But seek first the kingdom of God and

46

His righteousness, and all these things shall be added to you. 34 Therefore do not worry about tomorrow, for tomorrow will worry about its own things. Sufficient for the day is its own trouble.

My job was providing our health insurance and, at this point, the only funds to pay our bills. At the end of the day though, my job was competing for my time and complete attention. I had so little mental energy at this point in the journey; I had a decision to make. My first priority had to be staying in God's Will and serving my husband, as I had promised in my wedding vows many years earlier. The Bible is very clear about spreading yourself too thin and serving two masters.

Matthew 6:24 (NKJV)

24 "No one can serve two masters; for either he will hate the one and love the other, or else he will be loyal to the one and despise the other. You cannot serve God and mammon.

I had to take a step of faith and go on indefinite unpaid time off, trusting that God would provide. God uses people and situations to accomplish His will. And He did provide during this time - money, food, medical items we needed always appeared just when we needed them.

A few weeks after making the decision to put my job/career on hold, I worked with Human Resources at my employer on how to keep my insurance while on long term leave. That same day we received a check in the mail that we were not expecting. I had been in a car accident several months before Taylor was diagnosed with cancer. I was not hurt; it was just my car that had been damaged. I had pretty much forgotten about it with everything else going on the many months in between. The check was a result of the settlement from the other driver's insurance company. It was exactly the amount of money that we needed at that moment.

A consistent observation of mine throughout my life is - God is seldom early and never late.

STAYING STRONG IN FAITH AND WITNESS, REVISITED

It was one thing for us to realize that Taylor's death was closer than we had thought. It was a deeper struggle when we had to start thinking in terms of weeks and days. Even the strongest of people can start to question everything. Faith was becoming a daily purposeful act for us, sometimes hourly, at times even moment by moment. Faith is a choice.

Joshua 24:15 (NKJV)

15 And if it seems evil to you to serve the Lord, choose for yourselves this day whom you will serve, whether the gods which your fathers served that were on the other side of the River, or the gods of the Amorites, in whose land you dwell. But as for me and my house, we will serve the Lord."

Further, Taylor's To-Do list of short trips and household projects to ensure were getting done was winding down. This meant more idle time to just think. I could see changes in his body almost daily as the cancer took all that was good from his physical being. Faith, which had come relatively easy months ago, now required a daily concentrated effort. Taylor mostly wanted someone to read the Bible to him. I and several of his friends would tag team reading to him while he was awake. I also found a dramatized New Testament on CD[5] and set up a used stereo system with a 6 CD changer in his garage for him.

There was one section of Luke that Taylor requested repeatedly at this time.

Luke 12:4-7 (NKJV)

4 "And I say to you, my friends, do not be afraid of those who kill the body, and after that have no more that they can do. 5 But I will show you whom you should fear: Fear Him who, after He has killed, has power to cast into hell; yes, I say to you, fear Him! 6 "Are not five sparrows sold for two copper coins? And not one of

---

[5] *I highly recommend the CD set "The Word of Promise New Testament" (copyright ThomasNelson). I still listen to the set I bought for Taylor and I have bought others as gifts.*

them is forgotten before God. 7 But the very hairs of your head are all numbered. Do not fear therefore; you are of more value than many sparrows.

Taylor would make this first part very personal as he spoke it aloud with the reader - "Do not be afraid of the Cancer which kills this body, and after that can hurt me no more."

Luke 12:8-12 (NKJV)

8 "Also I say to you, whoever confesses Me before men, him the Son of Man also will confess before the angels of God. 9 But he who denies Me before men will be denied before the angels of God. 10 "And anyone who speaks a word against the Son of Man, it will be forgiven him; but to him who blasphemes against the Holy Spirit, it will not be forgiven. 11 "Now when they bring you to the synagogues and magistrates and authorities, do not worry about how or what you should answer, or what you should say. 12 For the Holy Spirit will teach you in that very hour what you ought to say."

Even as his own life was winding down, Taylor continued to try to be an encourager. I still remember how he would say "I am not strong, I am secure. There is a big difference. With security comes peace. I want you to be at peace."

TOGETHER WE BEGIN MAKING PLANS FOR MY FUTURE

We are instructed to walk through this valley... it does not say to stop and setup camp in the valley. We are not meant to linger in the valley. Taylor's desire for me was to keep moving forward, to make my way out of this valley of shadows and make it to the table prepared for me. It would be a long journey, but at that table would be the next chapter of my life. I would experience happiness and joy again.

Psalms 23:4-6 (NKJV)

4 Yea, though I walk through the valley of the shadow of death,

I will fear no evil; For You are with me; Your rod and Your staff, they comfort me.

5 You prepare a table before me in the presence of my enemies;

You anoint my head with oil; my cup runs over.

6 Surely goodness and mercy shall follow me all the days of my life; And I will dwell in the house of the Lord Forever.

Dropping permanently to one income would be a challenge. Like so many others, we had not prepared for one of us to die young. We didn't have a big life insurance policy to pay off the house and the rest of the bills. Looking back at our planning and our existing Will – we had to have that Will updated during this time – we realized that all of our planning assumed that we would die together. I don't think either of us ever consciously thought it, but the undertone of our previous planning seemed to focus on all of the time that we spent on the motorcycle together. We had travelled all over the east coast on a motorcycle. Before Taylor was diagnosed we had planned a multi-week trip all over South Dakota, Wyoming and Montana. I do regret that we never got to take that trip.[6] I even remember a conversation with our nieces several years earlier when they expressed deep concern that something bad could happen to us travelling so much on the motorcycle. We told them, as I remember it, "If we die together on the motorcycle, do not cry for us.

---

6 *Someday I hope to make that trip myself, although it would be in a car now.*

We were together doing something that brought us much joy and happiness. If we die at work, then you can cry… we were probably not joyful and happy then." Now we had to plan for me to continue on and start a new adventure, just like Ellie wanted Carl to do in the movie Up.

It would also be a huge challenge going from two people managing a household together, to one person. It would be easy to fall into worry and anxiety, to feel too overwhelmed to move. Taylor's desire, his expectation of me, was that I would stay focused on God, on my faith and on the promises of the future. He reminded me of a passage from Luke 12.

Luke 12:22-30 (NKJV)

22 Then He said to His disciples, "Therefore I say to you, do not worry about your life, what you will eat; nor about the body, what you will put on. 23 Life is more than food, and the body is more than clothing. 24 Consider the ravens, for they neither sow nor reap, which have neither storehouse nor barn; and God feeds them. Of how much more value are you than the birds? 25 And which of you by worrying can add one cubit to his stature? 26 If you then are not able to do the least, why are you anxious for the rest? 27 Consider the lilies, how they grow: they neither toil nor spin; and yet I say to you, even Solomon in all his glory was not arrayed like one of these. 28 If then

God so clothes the grass, which today is in the field and tomorrow is thrown into the oven, how much more will He clothe you, O you of little faith?

29 "And do not seek what you should eat or what you should drink, nor have an anxious mind. 30 For all these things the nations of the world seek after, and your Father knows that you need these things. 31 But seek the kingdom of God, and all these things shall be added to you.

He also reminded me of the passage I had used as part of my wedding vows. Taylor desired for me that I remain that "woman of great worth". He wanted me to continue in these promises that I made before God at our wedding.

Proverbs 31:10-31 (NIV)

10 A wife of noble character who can find? She is worth far more than rubies. 11 Her husband has full confidence in her and lacks nothing of value. 12 She brings him good, not harm, all the days of her life. 13 She selects wool and flax and works with eager hands. 14 She is like the merchant ships, bringing her food from afar. 15 She gets up while it is still night; she provides food for her family and portions for her female servants. 16 She considers a field and buys it; out of her earnings she plants a vineyard. 17 She sets about her work vigorously; her arms are strong for her tasks. 18 She sees that her trading is profitable, and her lamp does not go out at night. *19 In her hand she holds the distaff and grasps the spindle with her fingers. 20 She opens her arms to the poor and extends her hands to the needy. 21 When it snows, she has no fear for her household; for all of them are clothed in scarlet. 22 She makes coverings for her bed; she is clothed in fine linen and purple. 23 Her husband is respected at the city gate, where he takes his seat among the elders of the land. 24 She makes linen garments and sells them, and supplies the merchants with sashes. 25 She is clothed with strength and dignity; she can laugh at the days to come. 26 She speaks with wisdom, and faithful instruction is on her tongue. 27 She watches over the affairs of her household and does not eat the bread of idleness. 28 Her children arise and call her blessed; her husband also, and he praises her: 29 Many women do noble things, but you surpass them all." 30 Charm is deceptive, and beauty is fleeting; but a woman who fears the Lord is to be praised. 31 Honor her for all that her hands have done, and let her works bring her praise at the city gate.*

****

There was another thing that Taylor did as part of his planning for my life after his that surprised many people. He made an appointment with the Grief Center at Hospice to ensure there was a plan for moving me forward. When he first called and asked someone to come to the house,

Hospice responded that the Grief Counselors meet with the family after the death; there were other types of counselors available for the patient. He said that he understood that but he needed an appointment regardless. All those that knew my Marine know that he could be very strong willed when he had a goal to complete, and he usually got his way. They agreed to send a Grief Counselor to the house.

I had initially thought that Taylor had wanted to hear about the programs and counseling available for the family members through Hospice. I later found out that I was wrong on that assumption. When the Grief Counselor arrived the night of the appointment, she said "I don't remember ever meeting with a patient before. I usually get involved after the patient has finished the journey." Taylor looked at me and said, "Darling could you take the dog for a walk, maybe 20 minutes, please." So I left them in the family room to discuss whatever was on Taylor's mind.

I didn't find out until after Taylor was gone what they had discussed. At my first appointment after Taylor died, she told me some of what they discussed… it was all about me. She said not only had she never met with a patient before, she had never been requested to create a formal Grief Plan before. Taylor wanted to share with her where he felt my stumbling points would be after he was gone and to ensure that there was a plan on how she was going to help me move forward without him. There had to be a plan and he had to approve it while he was still here. God had truly blessed me with a husband that loved me more than I ever could have imagined.

THE HARDEST THING ABOUT THIS IS LEAVING YOU BEHIND... BEING WITHOUT YOU.

Toward the very end, Taylor said his greatest sorrow was leaving this world and moving on without me. He told me "I miss you when we are apart a week for a business trip. How can I leave here for God knows how long we will be apart?" I told him that, believing 2 Peter 3:8, he would not have time to miss me. By the time he saw Jesus and took in the awe of being present with the Lord, I would be along. For me it will seem like a thousand years, for him it will seem as a day.

He countered that I had to promise Verse 14... to stay in faith and in peace until I could join him in Heaven at my appointed hour.

2 Peter 3:8 and 14 (NKJV)

8 But, beloved, do not forget this one thing, that with the Lord one day is as a thousand years, and a thousand years as one day.

14 Therefore, beloved, looking forward to these things, be diligent to be found by Him in peace, without spot and blameless;

****

Because Taylor and I always thrived in finding the humor in almost every situation, here is a funny story…. Taylor shared these sentiments with his Social Worker from Hospice. She asked him if he had any regrets, anything he needed to make peace with while he still could. He told her that he really didn't want to die and leave me here; he wanted us to be together forever. She, apparently, became very concerned that he would try to "take me with him" and contacted a counselor to meet with us. We had an intervention of sorts… a long clarifying discussion about what Taylor meant by his comments.

TAYLOR'S FINAL GOAL

Taylor's final goal was, as he put it, "to stop existing on paper before I stop existing on earth". This meant he wanted to close all of his accounts, cancel all of his subscriptions, etc. while he was still able. He told me "You will have enough crap to deal with after I am gone. You don't need the headache of all this account management bureaucracy too." What amazed me though, and why I am including this, is the level of humor Taylor maintained during the completion of this goal.

Taylor had served with the 1/7 (1st Battalion/7th Marine) during his time in the Marine Corps. This meant he spent a lot of time training with the big 105mm Howitzer guns. They apparently really didn't do the whole ear-protection thing well back then, so Taylor had some hearing loss and a substantial amount of tinnitus from that time. This meant that he did not hear well over the phone when he held it to his ear, so the majority of his phone conversations were conducted on speaker phone. We got to overhear a lot of those calls.

I think the funniest one was cancelling the subscription to the newspaper. We really hadn't had time to read it for months and some were recycled right out of the delivery bag. Taylor told me "If you want to start reading the paper again after I am gone you can call and subscribe in your name." So he called Customer Service (CS), which, of course, wanted very much to find some way of continuing the subscription. The conversation basically went like this:

> Taylor: I need to cancel my subscription for the newspaper.

> CS: Is there some problem with the delivery that we can fix for you.

> Taylor: No, we just don't really have time to read it any more so we are going to cancel it for at least a little while.

> CS: Sir, if the daily paper is too much for you, I'd like to make you aware of our weekend only subscription. Would that better suit your needs?

> Taylor: No, thank you. Let's just cancel it.

CS: We also provide a Sunday only subscription.

Taylor: Thank you for your suggestions, but I also am planning for an upcoming move. Once I relocate I won't need the paper anymore.

CS: Sir, we do offer a service for those who move away from this area where we mail the newspaper to you for a small fee. You do end up getting Monday's paper on Tuesday, but you can stay in touch with local news in this area. Would that option be of interest to you?

Taylor: (phone on mute for a moment, comments to me – "This girl is good. She isn't giving up. One more obstacle for her." Smiles, and unmutes the phone.) Darling, thank you, really. But I am completely certain that the US Postal Service does not deliver mail to where I am moving. Thanks for trying. Now let's close this account.

I know that last comment went completely over her head and I'm sure she missed the humor in it. I had to leave the room so as to not be heard laughing in the background. It would have been easy for Taylor to get annoyed and go morbid with something like – "I'm dying.". That was not Taylor's style.

Taylor also kept his humor while canceling one of his Military Journals.

Taylor: I need to cancel my subscription please.

CS: OK Sir. Are you unhappy with the journal's content?

Taylor: No ma'am. I won't have a need to read it anymore soon. I'll get to view all of the action live where I am going.

CS: Are you being deployed?

Taylor: Yes, I suppose you could say that. Kinda changing units I guess. Reporting to a new duty station.

CS: I understand sir. I'll cancel that for you now. Please do your best to be safe where you are going.

Taylor: Ironically, I am reporting to the safest place in the universe.

I was so proud that Taylor kept his sense of humor and remained so upbeat during these conversations. He had a gift for humor.

There were many other conversations that went like those above. Taylor closed his retirement accounts, which, in case you don't know, you can do without tax penalty if your doctor certifies that you have less than 24 months to live. He closed all of his credit cards and requested to be removed from our joint accounts. (Some of those conversations were hilarious with quotes like "I don't think I'll ever need to buy anything on credit again." and "When you are preparing for the move I have coming up, your FICO score doesn't even come up, ever.")

Occasionally, I heard someone press him on his attempts at humor. This gave him an opportunity to share a little bit. He would include phrases like "We all die. I am thankful for the advanced notice. Not everyone gets that." I am so very proud of his faith and ultimate acceptance of what he could not control. His courage was a true blessing to me.

After he completed his move, when I went down to the Clerk of Courts to file his Will and process his estate, the clerk working with me even said "Do you know how blessed you are? This can often take hours and return visits to sort through. You will be done in less than 30 minutes. That man truly loved you." Yes, yes, he truly did.

GOD'S COMFORT DURING THE FINAL
WEEK OF TAYLOR'S TIME HERE

Taylor wanted to finish his journey here at home. He asked me to do everything I could so that he would die at our home. It was very important to him that it be just he and I together at that moment. I tried my best to have that for him. The brain swelling had started triggering seizures about a month before he died. At first we were able to control them with medications at home. Finally, over a matter of days, the seizures became more frequent and more severe than ever. I had been awake for almost 3 days straight just trying to manage his pain and his seizures.

During that third night, at one point he seemed to finally be asleep from the medications and the exhaustion of the seizures. I sat by the hospital bed Hospice had setup in the guest bedroom just days earlier quietly crying "T, I am doing everything I can and it isn't helping you. I am exhausted from trying to be nurse, cook, janitor, etc. I just want to be your wife for these last days. I just want to be your wife again."

The next morning when the Hospice nurse came into the house, Taylor asked to speak to her alone. When she came back out of the room she told me that Taylor had said "I can't keep putting her through this. You need to get me admitted to the Hospice Home now. I just need Velinda to be my wife again." Apparently, he had heard me cry during his sleep. It was such a comfort to me that he had made this decision; I would have done everything in my power to keep him at home and only cry when I was alone and/or he was sleeping. We ended up at a Hospice Home for the last eight days of his life.

****

In keeping with a consistent theme in our journey together, what should have been imprinted as a devastating memory became a funny memory. My parents had gone on a trip for an event and to see extended family about 6 hours away. Taylor had been very stable until that Friday night so there was no reason for them to put their plans on hold. I called them when the decision was made to move Taylor and they headed back home. In the meantime, Taylor's friend and current Commandant of their Marine Corp League detachment, Pete, came over to help me get things organized and closed up for our move. Our Hospice Nurse was also there attending to Taylor to get him ready for the trip – move him to portable oxygen, administer meds to make the trip easier on him, etc.

The medical transport vehicle was dispatched as soon as the Hospice Home had the room prepared for our arrival. For whatever reason, the transport showed up at the house with a gurney all decked out in pink sheets and a pink blanket. They may not have realized that the patient they were picking up was a Marine Corp Veteran; they should have at least noticed that it was a male patient.

When I answered the door all I could say was "Seriously… Pink?!? Pink bedding for my Marine? Seriously?!? Pink?" The transport tech said "When we drop off a patient we pick up clean bedding from there, whatever is on top of the stack, before we head out again. We don't carry extra bedding. Do you think it will be a problem?" I replied "Yes… yes, I do… but let's go see what happens."

I had tried my best during this entire illness to not let myself or others treat Taylor like an invalid. The nurse,

Pete and I would be able to help Taylor walk from the bedroom to the hallway and get onto the gurney. We could help him maintain his dignity during a time that probably felt like an overwhelming defeat to him. So I asked the transport techs to go only as far as the hallway. They really wanted to move him from one bed to the other, but, as it turns out, I can be just as stubborn as my Marine.

When they were in place with the transport bed in the hallway, the nurse and I went in to help Taylor stand up and walk to the gurney. Pete whispered to me, "You know this isn't going to go well…" When we got Taylor to his feet and he started pivoting toward the door, Taylor saw the bright pink sheets. He said "OH HELL NO!!" and sat back down.

Pete, in the true spirit of "Improvise, Adapt and Overcome" went to my linen closet and grabbed a set of queen sized tan flannel sheets and started covering the gurney mattress. He came back to Taylor and said, "Got you covered buddy, no more pink." We helped Taylor to his feet again and we walked to the now tan covered gurney.

I'm sure the transport tech was only thinking about the cold December evening air when he unfurled the Hello Kitty Pink blanket. My first thought was, "Crap! Which one of them is going to punch him first!" So I grabbed the flannel Marine Corp print blanket off of the bed, nudged (ok, maybe pushed) the guy with the pink blanket out of the way and covered Taylor in warm Marine Corp imagery.

My parents arrived at our house during the "Pink Fiasco". They finished locking up the house with Pete and took our dog to their house. I followed the medical transport vehicle to the Hospice Home. Instead of crying, I was laughing most of the way there – "Pink?!? Seriously?!? They brought PINK bedding! They thought they would wrap my Marine Veteran in PINK and he wouldn't notice?!? Seriously? Wow!"

****

It took almost 48 hours once we arrived at Hospice for the doctors and nurses to get the seizures to stop. I felt so helpless. I had to give up any illusions of control of this situation. I had to let go of my hold on my husband. You always wonder where your growth area will be when you go through a difficult trial. I heard words during that time that I never would have imagined being said about ME. One of the nurses said to me - "It is really admirable how you have been able to relinquish control and let go of his care, especially after being the one coordinating it for so long. You've transitioned better than most to being family, not primary caregiver, communicating your observations and letting us handle things... which is our job." ... Wait... I "relinquish control and let go"... I'm not sure that had ever happened before. In hindsight, God was helping me to let go of Taylor a little at a time.

The Friday before he left this earth, Taylor had a really good day. Numerous friends had come and gone all day and Taylor was in one of his humorous moods. We both laughed a lot that day. I knew that it is common for a terminally ill person to have a brief rebound of energy and life as the end draws near. I knew in my heart what this day probably was, but I forced myself to not think about that, to just enjoy this glorious day with friends and my soul mate.

Friday night, after everyone had left, Taylor asked me to come sit on the bed with him. He said "Today has been an awesome day. I am thankful for that. I also know that the end is very close now. I can feel it. I need you to not leave here again. I need you to be in this room now. Darling, I need your face to be the last thing I see before I see Jesus." Over the next 4 days, friends and family brought me food and beverages. There even a bathroom in the room. I did not have to leave the room.

Taylor did not speak again at all until Sunday morning. He did move his eyes responsively when people spoke to him. I don't remember what it was, but my Mom said something funny Saturday night in the room and Taylor rolled his eyes. He knew what was going on around him. He either was not able to, or choose not to, respond verbally.

Sunday morning, it startled me when Taylor spoke again. It was just he and I in the room. He said, "Darling, come sit with me. I am ready to go. I just need you to cut me loose." I did my best to reassure Taylor that I would move forward with my life. I would respect and honor his wishes for me. I knew it would be the hardest thing I had ever done, but I would do my best. Taylor went from looking at me to looking past me. His eyes brightened as he looked at the wall behind me. He said, "Oh darling! Look!" I did not turn around. I told him that whatever he was seeing was intended for him not me. If I turned around I would see a wall. I said "Whatever you are seeing, by the joy in your eyes, I'd bet it is beautiful." He replied, "I can't even speak." Those were his last word; he never spoke again.

God was faithful to the heart of Taylor's request. We would not be at our home, but everything else was exactly as Taylor had asked. Two days later, God allowed us to be alone together in the room during the last moments. The nurses were on a shift change; they were meeting to do that hand off of information about each patient. My parents were at a dinner at the American Legion. Taylor's sister and brother-in-law had called that afternoon to let us know they would not make it out to visit that night. I was sitting beside the bed talking to Taylor. I let Taylor know that both of our nieces were now done with their final exams for that semester; Taylor had been so concerned that he would mess up their semester. He slowly reached for my hand; I reached out and took his hand. Taylor turned his head toward me and looked into my eyes with so much love. He squeezed my hand. Then he cleared his throat; it almost sounded like a cough. And it was over. He never inhaled again. There was no struggle, no fight to draw another breath. Taylor was completely at peace. I sat there with him as his hand loosened its grip and his eyes became slowly distant. I had promised I would not do anything to intervene when the time came. I had promised to sit quietly with him. After about 5 minutes I put my other hand on his chest. There was no breathe and no heartbeat. It was indeed over.

I pressed the call button on the bed and asked for a nurse to come in. I told the attendant, "I'm pretty sure we are done now." The nurse came in and listened to his chest for the prescribed amount of time and "Called it". It was 7:28 PM Tuesday December 16th.

I sat with him a while longer with my head on his chest. Then I went out of the room to call family and friends while the nurses washed his body, removed all of the tubes and wires and covered him in the Marine Corp print flannel blanket I had made for him months earlier. He looked so peacefully asleep as family and friends gathered in the room that night.

****

What happened next had us all ending the night in laughter, as had always been Taylor's style. I will lay out this part in the order of events, as it happened that night.

The Hospice Coordinator called the funeral home to arrange for transport. When the driver arrived, we all stepped out of the room so that they could move Taylor's body from the bed to the transport gurney. All of the hospice employees and volunteers on site form an Honor Line, lining up on both sides of the hallway quietly while the body is moved from the room down the halls to the transport vehicle. I had stood with the family members of some of the others patients that passed before Taylor. So many people standing in reverence after the loss of your loved one actually does a lot to lessen the sting for that moment.

We all decided to wait until the man from the funeral left with Taylor before venturing out to our cars to leave. Frankly, I was not up to seeing the hearse leave the facility. The hearse driver came back into the Hospice Home, apologizing profusely. After he had loaded Taylor in the back and got in to leave, the engine would not start. He kept repeating "This has NEVER happened before."

My brother, being a mechanic, offered to take a look at the hearse while we waited on another vehicle to arrive. They couldn't find anything wrong with it other than the small issue that it wouldn't start. The lights were on strong so there was no issue with the battery. Nothing had come loose. We'd just have to wait a while.

Eventually another driver arrived in a Ford Cargo van. He came in and apologized to the family that the van was the only other vehicle available. While all of us, except my brother who was still trying to diagnosis the engine issue, waited in the room, they moved the gurney from the hearse to the van and the van left.

Then it hit me... but I was laughing too hard to share for several minutes. Taylor had always said, even before he was sick, "I did not live a sad, depressing life. My last ride will NOT be in a sad depressing hearse." And it wasn't. The bonus, I think, is that the second vehicle was a Ford Van; Taylor was a Ford man.

.

TAYLOR'S LAST RIDE

Taylor had bought a theme book around the time he decided to stop treatment. He kept notes in it about all of his planning and his final wishes for the funeral. Taylor and I had taken that notebook with us when we met with the funeral home many weeks before Taylor passed. The title he had written on the outside of that notebook was "Taylor Moore's Last Ride."

Yes, Taylor thought through all of the planning and exactly what he wanted. He even picked out and ordered his urn himself. This gift made things so much easier on his family. Really, all I had to do for the funeral was decide the day for the viewing and the day/time for the funeral and then show up to say a final goodbye. That was such a blessing.

Taylor wanted to be cremated, but it was also important to him to have an open casket viewing in his Marine Dress Blues first. He said he had been through both kinds of ending for friends and family and he thought it would give everyone, especially our nieces and myself better closure. He was then to be cremated wearing his Dress Blues.

For the funeral, he requested that it be held, not at a church (as he had said "church is for before you die, it won't do you a lick of good after"), but the American Legion building where he spent so much time. His military service and Veteran status were so important to him, second only to his faith.

To get from the funeral home to the American Legion, his urn was to be strapped down somehow on a motorcycle. There was to be absolute no hearse or other funeral home vehicles. The Patriot Guard Riders (PGR) were to be the escort and he wanted to ride with them. He said, "I've ridden with these guys. There are a lot of smart guys in that group. They will figure out how to secure a wooden box to a motorcycle." And they did. One of the guys rode a Trike that day and Taylor got to ride on the back seat with him. I rode on the back of one of Taylor's PGR friend's motorcycle, which rode just behind the trike. There were so many motorcycle there that day, not only from PGR, but also from Christian Motorcycle Association (CMA), American Legion Riders (ALR) and Rolling Thunder (RT).

Taylor had even left a map of the route he wanted PGR to take, which included riding past Faith Baptist Church and a few other landmarks important to him. We even had a police escort, which had to change at the county line. I am quite sure that Taylor was very pleased with this procession.

The funeral opened with the Marine's Hymn played on bagpipes and ended with Amazing Grace on the bagpipes. A fellow Marine and RT rider carried the urn from the Trike to the table at the front of the Legion Hall. Of course, military honors with the folding of the flag, the gun salute and taps were included. The Missing Man Table remained in its place in the front corner. Two friends from CMA played and sang Taylor's favorite hymn – "Leaning on the Everlasting Arms". Taylor requested that the service focus on two scripture passages, one from the old testament and one from the new testament.

Isaiah 43:1-2 (NCV)

1 Now this is what the Lord says. He created you, people of Jacob; He formed you, people of Israel. He says, "Don't be afraid, because I have saved you. I have called you by name, and you are mine.

2 When you pass through the waters, I will be with you. When you cross rivers, you will not drown. When you walk through fire, you will not be burned, nor will the flames hurt you.

2 Corinthians 5:17-19 (NIV)

17 Therefore, if anyone is in Christ, he is a new creation; old things have passed away; behold, all things have become new. 18 Now all things are of God, who has reconciled us to Himself through Jesus Christ, and has given us the ministry of reconciliation, 19 that is, that God was in Christ reconciling the world to Himself, not imputing their trespasses to them, and has committed to us the word reconciliation.

Taylor's final request for the funeral was an open microphone time for anyone who wanted to share a funny moment or story. He wanted his ending to be a reflection of the laughter and joy that had been his nature. And it definitely was a glorious send off.

MY FAITH JOURNEY - MY LIFE AFTER HIS DEATH

The topic of life after death comes up a lot after a major loss. If we are going to discuss "Life after death", we have to be clear: Are we discussing his life after his death? Or my life after his death? These are two very different discussions. This section is primarily about the latter - the things that were important to me as I moved forward.

You read earlier of my lessons about the valleys of life. I opened with that as, to date, they are still the most profound lessons I have learned during this journey. What follows are other lessons and personal growth from my part of continuing this journey.

This is by far more difficult to write about. During our shared journey, I had done a lot of journaling and a lot of reading of the Bible, both alone and with Taylor. I am sad to say that both practically stopped after the funeral. Reading the Bible went from a joy and an encouragement to a bitter-sweet memory. Journaling, too, became difficult. The feelings and emotions were way too raw to focus onto paper at that time. Even now, almost a year later, I struggle with putting this part of the journey into words.

Comparing the dips and rises during my first year as a widow to being on a rollercoaster would be a tremendous understatement. Moments of great happiness and joy would be immediately followed by great depths of sadness and grief that Taylor was not here to share the joy with me. There would also be an aspect of guilt – How could I be happy or joyful so close to Taylor's death? I loved my husband so much. Surely there was a minimum amount of time I should go without joy, right?

Wrong, even in the letters that Taylor left me, the constant theme was for me to find my joy again. Taylor wanted me to keep living, and in an odd way, to find joy that God had taken away all of his pain and suffering. If I could sum up the first year in one phrase, it would be "one huge emotional contradiction". I should be happy. I should be miserably sad. I remember my college roommate saying "Never should on yourself!".

While the first half of this book is chronological, this part is sectioned more into themes or struggles. I am figuring out this part as I share it with you. Honestly, I am still learning the lessons of the first year now as I look back on them.

THE GRIEF JOURNEY BEGINS LONG BEFORE THE CANCER JOURNEY ENDS

Our journey together ended on 12/16. While his journey through this world is complete, I am left to find my way through the rest of MY journey. It is important to realize that my grief journey began well ahead of Taylor's death. Over many months, I slowly lost the strong man that had been my best friend and my husband for so many years. His love and his spirit stayed strong even as his mind and body failed. The balance of our household slowly changed as I had to take on more and more of the responsibilities. In a way, the balance of our marriage roles shifted also.

The first passage that I struggled with as I settled more and more into the teacher role is found in 1st Timothy. I had accepted Christ as my Savior and began my lifelong faith journey 10 years before Taylor. I had been through more trials and challenges and times of study. I had memorized more scripture and been part of more small group Bible studies. Taylor had prayed to accept Christ while we were dating and was baptized before we got married. I often wonder now if he had done those things at least partially out of love for me and knowing me well enough to know I would have had issues entering into a serious relationship with a non-Christian. I don't want that to sound vain. At the same time, I am reminded of 1 Peter.

1 Peter 3:1-2 (NCV)

1 In the same way, you wives should yield to your husbands. Then, if some husbands do not obey God's teaching, they will be persuaded to believe without anyone's saying a word to them. They will be persuaded by the way their wives live. 2 Your husbands will see the pure lives you live with your respect for God.

Still, was God ok with a wife teaching her husband? I grew up hearing about the roles of men and women in the church. This one particular passage in 1 Timothy is pretty clear about women not teaching men.

1 Timothy 2:11-12 (NCV)

11 Let a woman learn by listening quietly and being ready to cooperate in everything. 12 But I do not allow a woman to teach or to have authority over a man, but to listen quietly, 13 because Adam was formed first and then Eve. 14 And Adam was not tricked, but the woman was tricked and became a sinner.

I struggled greatly with this. I called several of Taylor's male friends and let them know that Taylor was asking deep scriptural and faith questions and needed to talk with one of them. I am thankful to several Pastors and friends who helped me come to peace with my role of teacher and encourager to my husband. All asked me, in different ways, if Taylor was asking questions that I could not answer. I could answer his questions, but should I be "teaching" my husband? Then again, if he was asking me, he wanted to know what I knew. It would be better for him to have answers when he had the questions than wait and maybe not get the answers he needed? What did the Bible say about this topic in general?

I am always cautious about "single verse references" that are used to prove a point. The Bible must be understood as a whole. When I get into a debate where one side seems to be relying on a single passage for their argument, I like to share a "joke" about this sort of "Bible

Roulette" study: A man is distraught over his situation and decides he needs guidance. He determines that his best path will be to drop the Bible on the table and that the first verse his eyes fall upon will be the answer. So he drops the Bible and the first verse he sees is Matt 27:5 "And Judas went and hung himself." The man thinks, that can't be right. So he tries again. This time his eyes fall on Luke 10:37 "Jesus said to him, "Then go and do what he did.".".

So, back to my struggle with what could have been a "single verse reference" I remembered from childhood. I revisit the passage above from 1 Peter. In a way, this says that husbands can, and do, learn from their wife's faith.

I also went back to Proverbs 31:10-31. This was the scripture passage I had chosen for our wedding. Verse 11 says "Her husband has full confidence in her." Then in Verse 26 "She speaks with wisdom, and faithful instruction is on her tongue." This passage as a whole is about the role of a "wife of noble character". Taylor had full confidence in me. This was "faithful instruction". It was also deep discussion, not a lecture or a pedantic discourse.

In 1 Peter 3:15, we are instructed to "answer everyone who asks you to explain about the hope you have". Reading the whole chapter, it is clear to me that Peter is writing to both the men and women. He addresses wives and husbands in this letter.

1 Peter 3:15-16 (NCV)

15 But respect Christ as the holy Lord in your hearts. Always be ready to answer everyone who asks you to explain about the hope you have, 16 but answer in a gentle way and with respect. Keep a clear conscience so that those who speak evil of your good life in Christ will be made ashamed.

There was more reading and prayer as I challenged prior beliefs in this area. Again I am thankful to those who stood with me and helped me, including Zach, Pastor Dave and Pastor Leo. I am also thankful to God for allowing Taylor and I to share those special times of deep discussion and growth as I read scripture to my husband during this later phase of our journey together. Taylor grew in faith and wisdom and so did I.

MY COMFORT IN HIS FAITH

It makes me chuckle still when someone says something like "I'm sorry you lost your husband." I like to smile and respond "I didn't lose Taylor. I know exactly where he is. We are just in a bit of a long distance relationship until I get all my stuff finished here."

In all seriousness though, I am very thankful that I have no questions about my husband's faith. His profession of faith and his spiritual growth during this journey were obvious to all around him. I also take great comfort from what the Bible tells us happens to believers when the end of the earthly journey comes.

Taylor's tent wore out to a point of no repair. The vessel that contained him here on earth, the earthly home of his soul, simply expired. It was time for him to move on just like we are told in 2 Corinthians.

2 Corinthians 5:1-8 (NKJV)

1 For we know that if our earthly house, this tent, is destroyed, we have a building from God, a house not made with hands, eternal in the heavens. 2 For in this we groan, earnestly desiring to be clothed with our habitation which is from heaven, 3 if indeed, having been clothed, we shall not be found naked. 4 For we who are in this tent groan, being burdened, not because we want to be unclothed, but further clothed, that mortality may be swallowed up by life. 5 Now He who has prepared us for this very thing is God, who also has given us the Spirit as a guarantee.

6 So we are always confident, knowing that while we are at home in the body we are absent from the Lord. 7 For we walk by faith, not by sight. 8 We are confident, yes, well pleased rather to be absent from the body and to be present with the Lord.

As a Christian, we must recognize that our grieving here is for us, for ourselves. I cry because I am sad that I am without Taylor. I grieve my loss of seeing, feeling, touching him here, with me. I am not sad for him that he is not here. I would never ask him to come back to this world even if God made it an option. He finished his journey; his race is complete. That doesn't mean that I don't miss him terribly. Maybe the passage in 1 Thessalonians helps make this clearer.

1 Thessalonians 4:13 - 5:3 (NCV)

13 Brothers and sisters, we want you to know about those Christians who have died so you will not be sad, as others who have no hope. 14 We believe that Jesus died and that he rose again. So, because of him, God will raise with Jesus those who have died. 15 What we tell you now is the Lord's own message. We who are living when the Lord comes again will not go before those who have already died. 16 The Lord himself will come down from heaven with a loud command, with the voice of the archangel, and with the trumpet call of God. And those who have died believing in Christ will rise first. 17 After that, we who are still alive will be gathered up with them in the clouds to meet the Lord in the air. And we will be with the Lord forever. 18 So encourage each other with these words.

1 Now, brothers and sisters, we do not need to write you about times and dates. 2 You know very well that the day the Lord comes again will be a surprise, like a thief that comes in the night. 3 While people are saying, "We have peace and we are safe," they will be destroyed quickly. It is like pains that come quickly to a woman having a baby. Those people will not escape.

Death doesn't change who we are, just where we are. As a believer, whether we are alive or dead, we belong to God.

Romans 14:7-8 (NCV)

7 We do not live or die for ourselves. 8 If we live, we are living for the Lord, and if we die, we are dying for the Lord. So living or dying, we belong to the Lord.

IT IS NOT THAT I CAN'T DO IT, I JUST DON'T WANT TO

There are lots of verses in the Bible about Strength. I've quoted so many of them to so many people. I could probably create a verse-a-day calendar on Strength and another one on Fear. Oh, how I wish I could tell you that I read a bunch of passages and God strengthen me and all was well again. This struggle is not about trusting God to give me strength; God did give me strength. This struggle is completely about motivation; well, maybe a little bit about emotional exhaustion, too.

Taylor had taken care of so many day-to-day things during our marriage. This wasn't because I was not capable of doing them. He loved me and didn't want me to have to deal with them. Now, all of these things fell to me to either do, or at least manage. I did not have the energy or motivation to take all of that on. More than that though, I even lacked the motivation to leave the house. Even deeper, I lacked the motivation to get ready to leave the house. Just thinking about showering and getting dressed was exhausting. I had spent everything I had within me on being the caregiver.

So, it should have been a good thing when my employer offered to let me work from home for a while, right? Wrong. I know me. In fact, my quote is often "I know me. I've lived with me for almost 50 years!". If I didn't leave the house at that point, I never would. It would get harder and harder, not easier, over time. So I made myself do it. I made myself leave the house every day. Some days I cried all the way to work because I simply didn't want to go. I did not want to leave my comfortable fortress where I could pretend that nothing in my world had changed. Once I got to work I was fine.

I noticed at one point that Mondays were the hardest in the morning. So I figured, I would work from home on Mondays to make it easier on myself. Wrong again! The more consecutive days that I stayed in the house, the harder it was to leave. That first Tuesday it took anti-anxiety medication to get me to my car. What eventually worked for me was working from home on Wednesdays. This gave me a mid-week, one-day break from the emotional strain of leaving my comfort zone. A reward for pushing myself through for 2 consecutive days.

My lack of drive also contributed to me losing 50 pounds during the first nine months after the funeral. Very often my hunger level did not break the plane of motivation needed to do anything about it. If someone put food and utensils in front of me, I would eat. But I had no desire to walk to the kitchen, open the fridge and make a decision about what to take out. Something had to change. I had to do something.

One afternoon I was sitting on the couch whining to myself that my whole body hurt. (Yes, I hosted several pity parties for myself early on in this new journey, and I'm ok with that fact.) I knew that I had not eaten in a couple of days. So, I made myself, by utter willpower, go to the grocery store less than a half-mile away and buy food. I'm sure I looked like a mental case crying my way through the store, but I got food. I bought food that would take no thought – Fruit, nuts, granola, single-serving juice boxes, ready to eat popcorn and even Skittles. When I got home, instead of putting the food in the pantry, I put packages on every surface with a level top – night stands, end tables, kitchen counters, the desk and file cabinet in my home office, even on my desk at work. I would not allow myself to become so pitiful that I wouldn't open a bag of food sitting right next to me.

The bills the first month were also interesting. Every day I walked by the "Inbox" on the foyer table. It was always empty now. I kept thinking "some of the bills should surely be in by now. I hope the mail didn't get messed up by taking Taylor's name off things." Then one day another thought followed "Wait... Taylor... the mail. Taylor always got the mail." And he did. He would get the mail every afternoon on his way up the driveway. He would drop all of the bills in the Inbox in the foyer. I would get them from there once a week or so and pay them. The Inbox was empty for a month because it never occurred to me to go to the mailbox. Suffice it to say, I had a lot of mail to sort through that day.

Again, going to the mailbox everyday was not hard. It wasn't that I couldn't do it. I just really, really didn't want to do it. Taylor was supposed to do it. He was no longer doing anything to help out anymore. Just one more reminder that Taylor was gone.

The dog brought his bowl to me one day. I honestly couldn't remember the last time I had fed him. Taylor did that. Taylor fed the dog. "Dear Lord, Is everything my responsibility now?!? Was I expected to do everything I did before AND everything that Taylor had done?!?

Seriously?!?" The answer was, of course, "Yes." If I didn't take control of this, if I sat on the floor and cried every time I had to take on something that Taylor usually did, I would spiral into nothingness. Taylor wanted more for me than that. God wanted more for my life than that. Deep, deep down, I wanted more. I had to find the energy. I had to push forward every day as if my life depended on it… because basically, it did.

I worked on strategies with the Grief Counselors at Hospice. Remember that plan that Taylor had met with them about when he stopped treatment. Truth be told, Taylor's forethought in that area saved me from collapse. He knew me well enough to know I would not have been inclined to seek help. He had counseled many Veterans with the phrase "It takes the courage and strength of a warrior to ask for help." Taylor helped me to find that strength and courage by setting things in motion while he was still here.

One of the things that the counselors had me do was to work on lists. Some were practical lists – what needed to be done daily, weekly, monthly. I am a pretty organized person, a good planner. I just needed to get past the "overwhelming everything". I also made lists of my strengths, lists of things that Taylor and I did together, an abbreviated list from that one of things I still wanted to do, etc. We dug into my gifts for planning. All those who have worked with me know that I can create and work a "To-do" list as a planning tool.

We also worked on communicating "my needs" to my family and friends. I couldn't assume anyone else knew what was going on with me and what would help me most. Most of my friends had never been through this journey into widowhood. Even for the ones who had, every loss is different. I sent the following to family and friends, and it helped both them and me:

I have had so many decisions to make and so many responsibility changes recently that even seemingly simple things are often overwhelming. I need my "real" friends to take on a little more of the friendship responsibilities for a while as I heal and rebuild.

Please call me, text me, PM me, etc., don't wait for me to contact you. Yes, my phone can dial out, but not without energy and input from me. A year ago, walking across the room to get the phone, deciding who to call, finding the number and completing that action was no big deal. For perspective, at this point I have some nights that I don't eat because it requires more effort to go to the kitchen, decide what to eat, get it, heat/cook it and eat it than it does to just ignore hunger.

Please do not add to my "decision burden". I am making my decisions, decisions Taylor would have usually made and even more decisions with my recent unexpected employment changes. Every decision is another expense of my limited energy. Instead of saying "Let me know when we can get together." Try something like "I will be at _____ on _____. Wanna join me?" Or "I am making _____ for dinner tomorrow. I'd be happy to set a place for you if you can come."

Please continue to talk about Taylor and your memories of him. I need to maintain my connection to him and it is comforting to me that others still feel a connection. One of my best lunch dates in months, 3 of us spent a couple hours sharing stories and memories.

Please be patient with me. This is all so new and ever changing for me. I am in a new territory I never ever intended to visit. I will find my "new normal" soon... I have no time frame/ definition for the word "soon". I have even less definition/concept for the word "normal". I will get through this... with time. I hope all of you will still be here then.

No feedback to this is required or expected. Just for your awareness...

If I had to summarize this struggle in one phrase, it would be "How do you move a mountain? One pebble at a time."

SO, WHO AM I NOW?
CREATING/FINDING MYSELF AGAIN

I realized one day not too long after the funeral that this was not the first time I had questioned "So, who am I now?". I remember after college asking myself a lot of the same questions that I was asking myself now. I went back to my prayer journal from during that time right after college to look over the scriptures that were important to me back then. I do remember losing the whole "definition of self" when I finished college and became an "official adult". My "definition of self" had just taken another serious hit. I found the following passage that I had written and titled "Personal Observation" on the first page of my old prayer journal. I don't remember being this wise in my early 20's.

I cannot "find myself" by looking back at my past,
   nor by looking inwards to my feelings,
   nor by looking forward to my dreams,
   nor by looking at my current situation.
I will find myself by looking up,
for there I will find God
and He will show me the rest.

A lot about my life has changed since those early Post-College Days. I had become a wife. Over time, Taylor and I had stopped being Taylor and Velinda. We had become one flesh; we had become taylorandvelinda many years before now. Our identity had become the sum of our nicknames. We were TandTia. And then half of me started slipping away. Half of my heart, half of my identity, half of my future plans, half of ME was gone. A lot had changed, but one big thing had not changed. Who I am in Christ had not changed at all.

Romans 8:16-17 (NIV)

16 The Spirit himself testifies with our spirit that we are God's children. 17 Now if we are children, then we are heirs—heirs of God and co-heirs with Christ, if indeed we share in his sufferings in order that we may also share in his glory.

So the core of who I am had not changed, but I still needed to figure out which activities were primarily mine, which were ours and which were Taylor's. Which groups and organizations did I want to continue to be involved in? It was not only about what was me, what was Taylor and what was "us", it was also deciding, determining, which parts of that would move forward to the next phase of my journey as "Velinda". That, my friends, is still a work in progress.

There are a few things that changed within the first six months because I no longer had to take Taylor's preferences or likes/dislikes into consideration. Allowing myself these small changes brought peace and comfort that I did not expect.

I had grown up with pets. My parents had a dog when I was born. I can't think of a time longer than a few months when I did not have a pet. Growing up it was mostly dogs… Big Dogs. When I went off to college, more apartments accept small animals than large ones. I am not a fan of small dogs. (Neither was Taylor. He called them "ankle-nippers".) So starting in my 20's I became a cat-person. I had cats all the way up to not long before I met Taylor. When my favorite cat, ever, Clyde, died I didn't think I would ever get another cat again. That ended up ok though, because Taylor was allergic to cats. So on the six-month anniversary of being a widow I got a kitten... because I could.

I eat a lot of fish now. I love tuna, salmon, swordfish, etc. Taylor's idea of fish was a Filet-O-Fish sandwich. So any time I cooked fish for me I would have to cook something else for Taylor's dinner. Now I can have fish whenever I want. I can also have quinoa, kale, butternut squash risotto, etc. without having two meals cooking at the same time. It is good discovering (rediscovering?) these small things that are simply me.

I did lose half of me a year ago. Allowing myself to explore and grow the remaining half is what gives me hope for making the half that remains whole.

BECOMING THE HEAD OF MY NEW HOUSEHOLD

Every marriage is different. We all interpret the marriage scriptures a little differently. We take the marriages we were raised around into consideration - parents, grandparents, aunts/uncles, family friends. Our mix of personalities in the marriage plays a role as well. The only marriage that I really know deeply is my own.

For Taylor and I, Genesis 2:24 was very real. We became one flesh. We did not become one mind or one thought. We did become one unit together under God. Over time it did become harder to differentiate where one of us stopped and the other began. In some ways we did merge into one.

Genesis 2:24 (NKJV)

24 Therefore a man shall leave his father and mother and be joined to his wife, and they shall become one flesh.

I think a lot of non-Christians, and even some Christians, misunderstand the marriage principles of submission and leadership. Many women seem to think that "submitting to your husband" means a loss of self. Many men seem to think that submission from their wife gives them the right to be a tyrant and rule over their wife.[7] You really have to look at all of Ephesians 5, and some other passages to truly understand the Biblical principles for marriage. In order to explain my spiritual struggles with the loss of my husband, I really need to explain our understanding and practice of these principles.

---

7 *Quick story about not being allowed to become a tyrant... Taylor and I hadn't been married long when I commented that I was bored with my hair. I was thinking about making a change. I joked "maybe a big change... Maybe I'll change the color to something like little-kid-red hair." Taylor responded "I absolutely forbid you to dye your hair red!" I had only been joking about making that big a change to my hair; I was really considering something more like highlights. Guess what color my hair was 3 day later. Even though I didn't particularly like it on me, my hair stayed very red for several months. There is a line between leadership and tyrant and Taylor had crossed it. Just sayin'.*

Ephesians 5:1-2 lays the framework and perspective for the rest of the chapter. We are to "walk in the ways of love" using Christ's love as our example.

Ephesians 5:1-2 (NIV)

1 Follow God's example, therefore, as dearly loved children 2 and walk in the way of love, just as Christ loved us and gave himself up for us as a fragrant offering and sacrifice to God.

Many people want to start with Ephesians 5:22 in describing the roles in the marriage. I think that Ephesians 5:21 is too important to breeze over; it is deep in context. Submission goes both ways. We are to submit to each other in marriage; submission is a part of both the husband role and the wife role.

Ephesians 5:21 (NIV)

21 Submit to one another out of reverence for Christ.

One of the keys to consider is Christ's role as head of the church. Christ gave His life for the church; that is the love and commitment that is described for the husband.

Ephesians 5:22-33 (NIV)

22 Wives, submit yourselves to your own husbands as you do to the Lord. 23 For the husband is the head of the wife as Christ is the head of the church, his body, of which he is the Savior. 24 Now as the church submits to Christ, so also wives should submit to their husbands in everything.

25 Husbands, love your wives, just as Christ loved the church and gave himself up for her 26 to make her holy, cleansing her by the washing with water through the word, 27 and to present her to himself as a radiant church, without stain or wrinkle or any other blemish, but holy and blameless. 28 In this same way, husbands ought to love their wives as their own bodies. He who loves his wife loves himself. 29 After all, no one ever hated their own body, but they feed and care for their body, just as Christ does the church— 30 for we are members of his body. 31 "For this reason a man will leave his father and mother and be united to his wife, and the two will become one flesh." 32 This is a profound mystery—but I am talking about Christ and the church. 33 However, each one of you also must love his wife as he loves himself, and the wife must respect her husband.

So, back to my marriage... Taylor was the Head of the Household. We discussed almost every decision together. We both expressed our opinions, hesitations, concerns, etc. AND we both listened to the other's opinions, hesitations, concerns, etc. I would say that about 99% of the time we agreed on the course of action to take after these discussions. So what happened at the end of the discussion if we did not agree on a decision? After ensuring that we had both been heard and considered, if we still differed on what should be done, we went with Taylor's opinion. We discussed decisions together, but my husband had the final word in the event of a tie.

One of the hardest things for me after Taylor was gone was switching from talking with Taylor to talking with God directly on decisions that I now had to make. I had to slowly evolve from thinking/saying "Taylor, what would you say about this decision if you were here? I need to hear your point of view, your opinions, hesitations, concerns" to praying "God, What would You have me do in this situation?"

Don't get me wrong here. It isn't that I didn't pray before this point. Or that somehow Taylor had taken the place of God. We prayed together. Sometimes we would each pray individually and then come back together for more discussion. God was the ultimate authority, but Taylor was my counsel on earth. Taylor was the first person I called when anything major happened. I valued his opinion and his guidance.

But now, I couldn't call on Taylor. When a decision needed to be made for my household, I had the sole vote.

I could still ask other people for their opinion, but ultimately decisions for our household were now decisions for MY household. Even though we usually agreed, there is a comfort in knowing that my husband bore the brunt of the fallout if the decision that we made was not the best one.

My first major decision to face alone came less than a month after Taylor died. The day that I returned to work after my extended leave, a fairly big layoff was announced and my department was hit pretty hard. I had to make a decision between trying to find an internal transfer or taking a severance package. (Well, so much for the Grief Counseling advise to not make any major changes during the first year!) The first thing I did when I left my manager's office was to go to the lobby and try to call Taylor to tell him we really needed to discuss which way to go with this decision. His cell phone, of course, went straight to voicemail. I would have to make this decision, prayerfully, by myself.

Thinking back, maybe it was good for me to have such a major decision to make just out of the gate. It did sort of slap me upside the head with the realization that there would be a lot of big decisions coming up. I was smart. I could do this. Taylor and I usually agreed on the decisions anyway. Now I would just have to trust myself. And just like I had told Taylor when he had to make a decision about treatment – "Whatever you decide is the right decision and you keep moving forward. No looking back and no second guessing."

FORGIVENESS

At about six months after Taylor's death, the issue of forgiveness hit me hard, and unexpectedly. I finally got the strength to start cleaning up his garage. His garage was less about car storage and more about His Man Cave. That was HIS space. He had built and maintained a race car for five years in that space many years ago. He built models and bird houses out there. He hung out with his buddies to watch sports and war movies and drink beer. Again... Man Cave.

Most significant to my journey now, the garage was also the only place indoors he was allowed to smoke. This was a rule we agreed to from the very beginning of our house.

Cigarettes were often a point of contention in our marriage. I prayed for 17 years that God would help him overcome this addiction. I begged Taylor to try harder to quit. I bought him medications, patches, gum, hypnosis CD's, whatever the quit-smoking fad of the month was over those years. He'd stop for a while and then go right back. I thought being diagnosed with cancer would make him angry at the cigarettes and he would surely stop smoking. No. His reaction was more "The cow is already out of the barn. Why close the door now?"

The mixed-blessing - Taylor would always do everything in his power to make his wife happy. I was blessed with a caring and encouraging husband, a man of action who took care of things. He was also very much a pleaser deep down. He wanted me to be happy; he wanted to take away some of my stress. So he did his best to convince me that he HAD quit smoking. I knew better, but he tried.

So, back to cleaning the garage. I found packs of cigarettes - full, empty, half-empty - all over the place. I also found field dressed cigarette butts hidden inside, underneath, behind everything. I knew all along that he had not quit; I had accepted it. Or so I thought. Suddenly I was hit with feelings like - Anger: He lied to me. Jealousy: He choose those cigarettes over me. Frustration: We could have had more time together.

But wait... We started this cancer journey by going to Psalm 139:13-16 and Job 14:5. If God really had determined the number of Taylor's days while he was in the womb, did his smoking matter? Wouldn't the final outcome have been unchanged? Or was it that "the maximum number of days" were allotted and our actions can shorten that number, but not extend it? But in the end, God decided the date and time that each of us would die, right? Did I have any right, any justification, to be angry, jealous or frustrated?

One thing I have learned about emotions and feelings, things like "rights" and "justification" have extremely little to do with them. I could try to talk myself out of those feelings, but at the end of the day I had to accept my anger, jealousy and frustration. I had to take responsibility for them. I had to forgive the hurt that had been done to me. It did not matter if it was intentional or not; I know Taylor did not smoke to hurt me. But it did hurt me and I needed to forgive that hurt. I spent a while trying to convince myself that I was angry at the cigarettes. I had to accept that this was just not true. It was Taylor's choice, made of his own free will.

Scripturally I have noticed that forgiveness is often tied to compassion. It was out of compassion that God sent Jesus.

John 3:16 (NIV)

16 For God so loved the world that he gave his one and only Son, that whoever believes in him shall not perish but have eternal life.

It was out of compassion that both Jesus and Stephen prayed for their aggressors.

Luke 23:34 (NIV)

34 Jesus said, "Father, forgive them, for they do not know what they are doing."

Acts 7:59-60 (NIV)

59 While they were stoning him, Stephen prayed, "Lord Jesus, receive my spirit." 60 Then he fell on his knees and cried out, "Lord, do not hold this sin against them." When he had said this, he fell asleep.

We too are called to compassion and forgiveness.

Colossians 3:12-13 (NIV)

12 Therefore, as God's chosen people, holy and dearly loved, clothe yourselves with compassion, kindness, humility, gentleness and patience. 13 Bear with each other and forgive one another if any of you has a grievance against someone. Forgive as the Lord forgave you.

Ephesians 4:31-32 (NIV)

31 Get rid of all bitterness, rage and anger, brawling and slander, along with every form of malice. 32 Be kind and compassionate to one another, forgiving each other, just as in Christ God forgave you.

Forgiving Taylor now for his actions that contributed to my hurt would do nothing to benefit him. Letting go of the hurt, anger, frustration and bitterness would benefit me. It would benefit my relationship with others and with God. Forgiveness is a choice. It is extending grace to others even as God has extended grace to you.

Ephesians 4:26-27 (NCV)

26 When you are angry, do not sin, and be sure to stop being angry before the end of the day. 27 Do not give the devil a way to defeat you.

Luke 6:37 (NIV)

37 "Do not judge, and you will not be judged. Do not condemn, and you will not be condemned. Forgive, and you will be forgiven.

This last verse was probably the most enlightening for me. At the end of the day, my anger was anchored in judging Taylor's actions. I knew his heart; I knew his true intentions. That did not matter. My hurt came from my expectations. If he loved me more he could have quit. If he cared about my feelings, he would not have lied about quitting. He would not have tried to deceive me.

Working through this, praying through this, flipped the coin for me. I found myself crying out "Taylor, forgive me for being angry, judgmental and condemning of your actions. I inserted intentions and motivations into your actions that contributed to my hurt. You could not have known at 14 the impact and interruptions cigarettes would have on your life." and "God, I am angry because I am alone. It was not my plan for my husband to die at this point in my life. Forgive me for blaming my husband for this loss. Forgive me for being angry that my life did not go according to my plan. Restore in me compassion, forgiveness and acceptance of Your Will for my life."

JOB'S FRIENDS WERE ALSO JUST TRYING TO HELP...

I struggled deeply with whether to include this chapter or not. My goal, as I stated earlier, is genuinely to try to help others with what I have learned in this journey. This section is not easy to discuss, so many people will be hesitant to brooch the subject. Take note: Being a Widow/Widower is not for Sissies.

I also want to state clearly: I truly believe that each person had my best interests at heart and really believed they were helping me. Even Job's wife and friends tried to be helpful. Further, you never really completely understand what is going on in someone else's heart or mind.

****

117

During the last few weeks of Taylor's life, I had a recurring dream. It was a dream, though in reality it should have had the disturbing impact of a nightmare. Partially because I was disturbed that the dream was NOT disturbing, and partially because of our horribly wrong cultural norms on this subject, I did not share the dream with anyone for close to a year.

Remember that the goal was for Taylor to die at home. He really wanted it to be a comfortable transition in our home with just he and I together. In the dream, that is what happened. I awoke to find that Taylor had slipped away in his sleep. Without any emotion at all, I got out of bed, walked down the hall to the kitchen, poured a glass of water and took all of the morphine that was left. I then went back to bed and snuggled up next to Taylor and fell asleep. Each time I woke up from this dream, I was surprised to find we were both still alive.

I don't think I was really suicidal at the time. I wasn't thinking about it or planning anything while I was awake. I do think that others would have freaked out if I had shared the dream. I believe that dreams are thoughts and feelings that your conscious mind cannot handle addressing. I think deep down I was feeling that after

Taylor died, I, myself, would just be waiting to die. So much of my life was ending, what would be left?

I did have the clearness of thought to ask the Hospice Nurse that had been coming to the house to remove all of the medicines from the house when we moved to the Hospice Home. I didn't ever fear doing anything while I was awake. I was concerned about sleep walking or some other means, like exhaustion, causing my subconscious to take over.

So, understanding more about my state of mind, which no one but me did at the time, you will better understand the ministering that was not helpful to me. A big one was hearing, over and over, "When you die, you and Taylor will be together again." Off and on for many months, it felt like other Christians were selling death as an option. For instance, "Just like Taylor, when you leave this world you are promised a perfected body with no more tears and no more pain. These tears and pain will not last forever; Heaven awaits you." That was a promise and a comfort for the future. I needed promises and comforts for now; comforts that would ease the pain here and not make heaven look like such a great short term option. I heard this passage quoted a lot.

2 Corinthians 4:17 – 18 (NCV)

17 We have small troubles for a while now; but they are helping us gain an eternal glory that is much greater than the troubles. 18 We set our eyes not on what we see but on what we cannot see. What we see will last only a short time, but what we cannot see will last forever.

Yes, all of this is true; but is it helpful in this situation? A huge part of my life had been ripped away from me. I had a very loose grasp on what was left. Christianity is more than a promise of the afterlife; otherwise, why not just die after conversion? I had to dig in prayerfully and find my way to a peace for now, a peace that was greater than waiting to die so we could be together again. Plus, the real goal of my faith was not to reunite with Taylor. The goal of my faith was to reunite with Christ as Taylor had just done.

So here are some things that were very helpful to me. Let's start with the fact that God is with me now. I do not have to wait until after death to feel God's presence and guidance. In Matthew 1, as well as in Isaiah 7, we read that "God is with us".

Matthew 1:23 (NKJV)

23 Behold, the virgin shall be with child, and bear a Son, and they shall call His name Immanuel, which is translated, "God with us."

We are called to be "in the world, but not of the world". Our place is here until God decides to bring us home. This is where I am supposed to be for now. Right before Jesus was betrayed, He prayed for the disciples and also for future believers. He declares that He, Himself, has sent us into the world.

John 17:11-21 (NCV)

11 I am coming to you; I will not stay in the world any longer. But they are still in the world. Holy Father, keep them safe by the power of your name, the name you gave me, so that they will be one, just as you and I are one. 12 While I was with them, I kept them safe by the power of your name, the name you gave me. I protected them, and only one of them, the one worthy of destruction, was lost so that the Scripture would come true.

13 I am coming to you now. But I pray these things while I am still in the world so that these followers can have all of my joy in them. 14 I have given them your teaching. And the world has hated them, because they don't belong to the world, just as I do not belong to the world. 15 I am not asking you to take them out of the world but to keep them safe from the Evil One. 16 They don't belong to the world, just as I do not belong to the world. 17 Make them ready for your service through the truth; your teaching is truth. 18 I have sent them into the world, just as you have sent me into the world. 19 For their sake, I am making myself ready to serve so that they can be ready for their service of the truth.

20 I pray for these followers, but I am also praying for all those who will believe in me because of their teaching. 21 Father, I pray that they can be one. As you are in me and I am in you, I pray that they can also be one in us. Then the world will believe that you sent me.

That is a long passage. Jesus is praying for us, for not just the current believers at that time, but also for those who will later believe. It is awesome to consider that Jesus prayed for us. With that in mind, read through it one more time with particular emphasis on verses 13 "so that these followers can have all of my joy in them.", 14 "I have given them your teaching.", 17 "Make them ready for your service through your truth; your teaching is truth", 21 "Then the world will believe that you sent me"

What am I supposed to do while I am still here? Serve. At times after Taylor dies, I felt like I had given it all away. It felt like I had nothing left to give. But I do. God says that He renews my spirit every day. Earlier I mentioned that I heard 2 Corinthians 4:17-18 a lot as a promise of what was to come when I was done here on earth. Never pick and choose verses out of context with the rest of the chapter, the rest of the book, even the rest of the Bible. If only they had started ministering to me beginning a verse earlier.

2 Corinthians 4:16 (NCV)

16 So we do not give up. Our physical body is becoming older and weaker, but our spirit inside us is made new each day.

I encourage you to read the entire book of 2 Corinthians; it is a pretty short book. For the sake of brevity, I want to skip ahead to Chapter 5, verse 6.

2 Corinthians 5:6-10 (NCV)

6 So we always have courage. We know that while we live in this body, we are away from the Lord. 7 We live by what we believe, not by what we can see. 8 So I say that we have courage. We really want to be away from this body and be at home with the Lord. 9 Our only goal is to please God whether we are here or there, 10 because we must all stand before Christ to be judged. Each of us will receive what we should get – good or bad – for the things we did in the earthly body.

So, my purpose while I am here being not only to Serve, but to serve in a way that is pleasing to God. Romans 14 phrases it a little bit differently.

Romans 14:7-9 (NCV)

7 We do not live or die for ourselves. 8 If we live, we are living for the Lord, and if we die, we are dying for the Lord. So living or dying, we belong to the Lord. 9 The reason Christ died and rose from the dead to live again was so he would be Lord over both the dead and the living.

I found a lot of hope for this life in the Scripture. It was this hope for NOW that I desperately needed which God supplied through His Word. I think it will also help me in ministering/witnessing to others' "hope-needs" to be in this moment, as well as in the future. Just a few more passages that really helped me.

God promised to give me strength and power to get through this time, even the strength to rise above it.

Isaiah 40:29-31 (NCV)

29 He gives strength to those who are tired and more power to those who are weak. 30 Even children become tired and need to rest, and young people trip and fall. 31 But the people who trust the Lord will become strong again. They will rise up as an eagle in the sky; they will run and not need rest; the will walk and not become tired.

God promised to give me peace, a peace that surpasses all understanding.

Philippians 4:4-7 (NCV)

4 Be full of joy in the Lord always. I will say again, be full of joy. 5 Let everyone see that you are gentle and kind. The Lord is coming soon. 6 Do not worry about anything, but pray and ask God for everything you need, always giving thanks. 7 And God's peace, which is so great we cannot understand it, will keep our hearts and minds in Christ Jesus.

My life is a gift from God and an offering back to Him. Taylor had finished his race. He had fought to the end and stayed faithful. My race is not yet over. God has more for me to do here. I do not know what my "mission" may still include; I just know that I need to be open to whatever remains for me to do.

2 Timothy 4:5-7 (NCV)

5 But you should control yourself at all times, accept troubles, do the work of telling the Good News, and complete all the duties of a servant of God. 6 My life is being given as an offering to God, and the time has come for me to leave this life. 7 I have fought the good fight, I have finished the race, I have kept the faith.

Acts 20:24 (NCV)

24 I don't care about my own life. The most important thing is that I complete my mission, the work that the Lord Jesus gave me – to tell people the Good News about God's grace.

I have one more issue with advice that was not helpful. Since I was taking medication for depression and anxiety, I was told by some well-meaning individuals that my "thinking wasn't right" and also that I wasn't trusting God. I promise you that it is not helpful to try to make someone feel guilty or shame over emotions like deep sadness, depression, or anxiety. God addresses depression and anxiety and even anger. He knew we would have these emotions and gave us guidance on how to deal with them. It would have helped me tremendously to have heard that these emotions were ok, so long as I dealt with them as God instructed. Instead several Christians caused me to feel like I was somehow sinful or unfaithful over the deep sadness of losing my spouse. God's word says something different. In 1 Peter, God acknowledges our anxiety in times of trouble. He also tells us that, in time He will restore our strength to us.

1 Peter 5:6-11 (NIV)

6 Humble yourselves, therefore, under God's mighty hand, that he may lift you up in due time. 7 Cast all your anxiety on Him because He cares for you.

8 Be alert and of sober mind. Your enemy the devil prowls around like a roaring lion looking for someone to devour. 9 Resist him, standing firm in the faith, because you know that the family of believers throughout the world is undergoing the same kind of sufferings.

10 And the God of all grace, who called you to His eternal glory in Christ, after you have suffered a little while, will Himself restore you and make you strong, firm and steadfast. 11 To Him be the power for ever and ever. Amen.

God says to cast all of your anxiety on Him. He doesn't chastise us for feeling anxious. We are warned to not lose faith during the time of suffering. Note that God does not say that if we cast our anxiety on Him that He will immediately take it all away; know that the suffering may last a while. If we remain faithful, God promises to restore us in His time.

Psalms 94:18-19 (NKJV)

18 If I say, "My foot slips,"
Your mercy, O Lord, will hold me up.

19 In the multitude of my anxieties within me,
Your comforts delight my soul.

Proverbs 12:25 (NKJV)
25 Anxiety in the heart of man causes depression,
But a good word makes it glad.

There are two places an anxious person can get a good word. One is going to the Word of God prayerfully during times of anxiety. The other is from other people; take caution that you weigh the words of others against the Word of God. The latter is the ultimate truth.

Here are some words of truth from others that were comforting to me:

"God sees your struggles and He will restore your strength."

"God knows your suffering. Just as you were with Taylor through his pain, God watched His own son go through terrible pain. He saw His own son Jesus die on the cross. Trust that He understands what you are feeling and will renew your spirit daily."

ON FRIENDS AND RELATIONSHIPS

It took about six months before I woke up enough to really think through getting back to doing any of our usual activities. It was struggle enough to go to work and eat meals during the first months. (We've already discussed that earlier.) It wasn't until I started contemplating going to meetings or other activities we had shared that I thought much about friends and changes in relationships.

I said earlier that after Taylor was diagnosed God surrounded us with friends who helped and encouraged us. The first week or so after Taylor died I was also surrounded by a lot of friends. And then Christmas week started. All of these friends had other friends and family, and a life of which I was only a very small portion. For the next few weeks, most people entered back fully into their own lives… as well they should. Going through this time and also hearing comments from some others who had been through the same fluctuations in friends really made me think through the whole topic of friends and relationships.

I have been very attentive to not trying to give advice in this book. I want to just share with you what worked for me. Forgive me this one transgression to that goal now. When it comes to friends and changes over time, please do not allow yourself to get bitter. Step back and try to understand both sides of the changes – yours and theirs. Maybe my experiences here will give others a new perspective.

Before Taylor and I met, we were both individuals with our own lives and interests. (As my sister Julie would say "Thank you Captain Obvious".) When we started dating we were both open to the interests of the other. Taylor brought me NASCAR, Cary Grant movies, motorcycles and spontaneity. I brought him Symphony, Community Theater, folk music, NCAA Basketball and the ability to turn any task/activity into a detailed project plan. As our interests merged, so did our friend list. But why?

A lot of friendships are based on common interests. That is their core foundation. And when that foundation changes, so often does the core of the relationship. Some friends fall across several interests, which is better for the long haul. Looking back, we had motorcycle friends, church friends, theater friends, race friends, work friends, military friends, etc. So it was not surprising to me that some of these friendships changed dramatically after Taylor moved on from this world.

We had a large circle of friends that we rode with and travelled with all over the east coast. These weren't "my husband's friends", or "my friends", they were our friends. And then our motorcycle and my driver were both gone. I really couldn't do these trips anymore. I tried a few in my car following motorcycles, but it was not at all the same thing. A few of our single friends offered to let me ride on their motorcycle with them. But on a motorcycle the rider/passenger interaction is a very intimate way to travel. The rider and passenger maintain constant contact and act as one on the motorcycle. It isn't as simple as riding in the passenger seat of someone's car. These friendships suffered. They all still travelled together; their lives did not change as significantly as mine did, and they shouldn't have changed.

Then there were church friends. I couldn't go back to the same church Taylor and I had been attending. Just parking in the parking lot reduced me to tears. So Shawna and I started visiting other churches and just sort of floated around for many months. We met new people.

We weren't in one place long enough to bond with many new friends though.

There are work friends. These often revolves around a central geographical location and a common goal of an employer. You can go to lunch easily because you are already together at lunch time. You can plan after-hours get-togethers easily because you see each other almost every day. I still meetup with my work friends even though we no longer work together. I still consider them all as friends. But, in-person interactions get harder and require more energy and planning.

The military friendships were trickier. Taylor was often referred to as "a Marine's Marine". "For God, Corp and Country" was not a catch phrase for Taylor. Those words were who he was to his core. While he was sick, his "brothers" handled so many things. After he was gone, several continue to this day to check on me and help out where I need help. They are helping "their brother's widow". There were also some who did not handle Taylor's death well at all. I remember a few coming to me individually to express basically the same sentiment. Paraphrasing the conglomerate – "I really feel like I should be there for you. Taylor would expect me to take care of things even as he would have done for my family. But, honestly, every time I see you without Taylor, it is like getting punched in the gut again. Like getting smacked upside the head by the fact that Taylor is gone." Yes, I lost a husband, best friend, soul mate. But they also suffered a huge lost. They lost a best friend, a brother in arms. It would be easy to make this whole journey about me and MY loss. In reality there were a lot of people who lost Taylor. Each of them needed time and space to navigate their own journey.

There are several people from our "previous" friends group that I still talk to and see occasionally. I even try to make new friends now but it is hard putting myself out there. Another thing I shy away from is surrounding myself with fellow widows. I have several friends who are widows and I find that the dynamic there is a thing of its own. There are a few widows who are much further along in this journey than I am. They are an encouragement to me and I enjoy our time together. They give me wisdom, perspective, hope. I give them someone to help through the part of the journey they have already completed. I also have a few new friends who are very new to this journey. To them, I am the old pro. I give them hope, perspective and a non-judgmental ear to listen. All they have to give me is the opportunity to help someone walking behind me in this valley.

I am however cautious to not surround myself completely with widows. I don't want to become only, as my friend and fellow widow Kate puts it, "the ol' widder Tia". When I was married, I went out with the girls. Some were married and some were single. I need a diverse set of women friends again.

Some of my longtime friends are still longtime friends. Some of my new friends may become longtime friends as we move forward. Just remember the adage – "People come into your life for a reason, a season, or a lifetime.". The flip side of that is often missed – YOU come into other's lives for a reason, a season or a lifetime.

Before you judge those who you perceive to have left you, consider all of the times when you have moved away for one reason or another, or even unintentionally for no reason at all.

FINAL THOUGHTS

As you can tell, this book took me the better part of a year to write. At times, reliving the journey became overwhelming emotionally and I had to step away for weeks at a time. My sources are not only my memories, but also rereading my journals and my prayer journal. There are also all of the passages that Taylor marked in his Bible and the most worn pages from the passages that Taylor requested to be read aloud most often.

This has truly been a journey. While I have emerged from the deepest places of this valley, my journey continues and I must move forward. Only God knows what my future holds. I do know this - it is impossible for God to direct my steps if I refuse to move my feet. I believe that God uses those who have travelled the valleys to help guide those who enter the same valleys after them.

My only prayer for this book is that others will also see the presence of God in this journey and be blessed by it. My hope is that it will help others to find strength and peace and may even help those who find themselves ministering to the struggling.

ABOUT THE AUTHOR
By George Tracy

When Velinda Moore approached me about writing a few words about the Author, I was very hesitant, even though I have known her for 49½ years. The only one to know her longer would be her mother, who knew her in the womb.

I will not bore you with all of her formative years except to say she was a precocious child who enjoyed life to its fullest and was very studious and had a real grasp of technology. While in high school (graduating Salutatorian) she learned to program in "Basic" and wrote her first game - Battleship. She graduated from New College, in Sarasota, Florida, where she received her Bachelor of Arts with dual majors in Biology and Psychology. She spent the next year working at the college setting up and expanding their computer network.

After being excepted into a Doctorate program in Neuroscience at the University of Oregon, it was off to Eugene. It was discovered during this time period, while working with a barn owl (named Barnie), that she had an aversion to euthanizing avian and mammalian lab subjects. Also, a professor noted that it appeared she enjoyed the programming side of her research more than the medical side. After releasing the barn owl back into the wild, she took a hiatus to explore her software side and never looked back.

She held numerous programming positions with Real Estate Report Generating startups and Insurance companies before going back to school to become a Medical Technician. This lead to working as a phlebotomist in the trauma unit of a hospital in South Florida and at numerous labs. Then she combined these two backgrounds to begin working in Information Technology (IT) at medical equipment companies in North Carolina. It was during this time that she met and married the love of her life Albert Taylor Moore and made another career change by going into banking IT and quality assurance.

I say all of this just to show that we have no idea of where God will lead us in life or what we will be called upon to do. While Velinda is not a Theologian (she would be the first to point that out), she has studied the Bible as an individual believer. Also, she and Taylor did do bible studies together. It was through those times, at the end of Taylor's life, that she has been inspired to write about. Things that helped her (and him) cope with the inevitability. It is hoped that this book will give encouragement to others who are facing like circumstances.

30396980R00083

Made in the USA
Middletown, DE
22 March 2016